MY ABERRANT MIND

MY ABERRANT MIND

A Spiritual Rags to Riches Journey

KRISTIN DOLCE
Kadesha Powell, MarZe Scott

Kristin Dolce

ACKNOWLEDGEMENTS

I have had a heaven-sent team of beautiful people that have made this book possible. Firstly, gratitude to Source for directing me to my purpose.

I would like to give thanks to my husband, Jeremy Dolce, for having faith in me and encouraging me through this emotional and tedious process.

I appreciate the time and dedication of a group of beautiful women. Thank you to my lady's at Connecting Consciousness and Big Island Writer's Group for having faith in me and pushing me to keep going.

Last but certainly not least I could not have done this without my extraordinary writing team. My developmental editor MarZe' Scott from KeLaCar Enterprise and my content editor, author and book coach, Kadesha Powell, at KadeshaPowell.com You have both gone above and beyond for me. I do not see you as co-workers, but as friends.

I dedicated this book to Bart Taylor.

You have truly been my angel in human form. You saw a light in me even when I was lost in the dark. I'm Forever grateful for everything you have done for me over the last 16 years.

INTRODUCTION

We are born into this life with a variety of gifts and talents. Some are blessed from the door with the knowledge to remember; for the rest we must carefully put together the pieces of who we are truly meant to be. In order to remember we go through a series of tests and trials, of obstacles and triumphs; a spiritual initiation so to speak.

This is my raw and exposed truth of who I'm and how I became the resilient woman I'm today. I must warn you that some parts may be explicit and triggering. So please only read when you are ready to start your healing journey. My story may cultivate memories of situations in your life that are yet to be resolved.

I start this trip with you to show you that anything is possible; to give hope to those filled with guilt, shame and confusion. While sharing and exploring with you it allows me to continue to heal. Please follow with imagination and an open mind. Right behind the door of madness is where the magic begins. Enjoy the ride.

P.S. Out of respect for others some names have been changed. For today I understand they were just roles being played for my ultimate success. The only way one can ever experience the light is by first going through the dark.

ABOUT THE AUTHOR

Kristin Lee Dolce is a true Jersey girl, born and raised in the borough of Somerdale, but is now an authentic mountain mama. Newly married to her soulmate, Jeremy, and the mother of seven. The family is in the modest country town of Big Island in the Blue Ridge Mountains of Virginia.

Always a writer at heart, Kristin was first published in "A Sea of Treasures", a poetry anthology distributed by the National Library of Poetry in 1995 at the tender age of sixteen. Kristin often performed spoken word, in her younger years, at local theaters, and coffee shops.

Nowadays, she loves to garden and is learning to homestead. She possesses an inquisitive mind, and a delicate but genuine heart. She has become a pathfinder for souls and loves to share her exploration, experience, and knowledge with others through her writing.

TABLE OF CONTENTS

My Aberrant Mind ©2023 by Krisitn Lee Dolce
Published by Kaydee Travels and Media LLC
Trade Paperback ISBN 978-1-7366562-3-5
E-Book ISBN 978-1-7366562-4-2

Cover design: Bookcoverzone.com
Editorial Team:
Kadeshaq Powell, KadeshaPowell.com
Marze Scott, KeLaCar Enterprises, marzescott@gmail.com

First Printing, 2023

CHAPTER 1.1 EARLY YEARS

Part 1 My Story

Grand rising, my beautiful souls. Let's travel back in time to the Spring of 1978.

Let me start by saying that my mom still has the knife from the day we escaped a life of turmoil from my father. She sleeps with it on the table, next to her bed for protection. This symbol is the beginning of a journey of twists and turns, the path of which made me who I am.

I was born in South Jersey to two teenage parents Daisy and Ricky. Daisy had just celebrated her sweet sixteen a month to the day on March eleventh and Ricky would turn nineteen on August eleventh. I was born on April eleventh. That's a lot of elevens. This has always fascinated me. I knew there was something to it, just uncertain what it was.

Being a teenage parent is a struggle for anyone. They decided they were going to give it their best shot at starting a family. When I was a year old, they got married as society said you're "supposed" to do. They rented a small apartment in a suburban town called Magnolia, New Jersey. It was one town over from where they were both raised in Somerdale.

Neither of them were fully ready for the dedicated effort it takes to make a marriage work. Who really is at this age? Ricky struggled with addiction and severe anger issues. He was still discovering who he was as a person and had his own battles to face.

My mom was only a sophomore. This meant dropping out of school and having to learn to be a mother and wife way before she was ready.

Living with my dad's problems made it dangerous for us to stay. There was one instance where my grandmother walked in while he had a pillow over my face, suffocating me because I wouldn't stop crying. Then there was the time my mother, and I were chased from our apartment to my grandparents as my father wielded a machete. I was small enough that I rode in a stroller.

Even though she had no money to feed or care for me, nor a place of her own, and no real options for stable income, my mother took him to court for sole custody.

They advised her that no judge would take away a father's parental liberty. She was told a child deserved to have a relationship with her father. Ultimately, child support was ordered, and they granted him visitation, but it all seemed senseless considering what became a consistent disappointment.

Week after week, I faced an imminent letdown. Sitting on our back steps, I would tuck my head in my white crocheted shawl and cry— I wanted him to show up so badly. I could hear the echoes of the adults derisively remarking on how they knew he wouldn't come. Their caustic words only exacerbated my sentiments; I desperately needed everyone to be wrong.

My still developing mind said that I wasn't important enough to want to spend time with. In retrospect, it was my dad who could not love himself. However, to my little heart, it felt as though he didn't love me. Often we dismiss the importance of family and its lasting impact.

He missed so many visits that when he was taken back to court; he lost his rights to see me all together. I understand they did this, it was for my safety. In my mind, there could've been an alternative resolution. His absence, no matter how dangerous they said he was, left me with an empty place in my heart at an extremely young age.

We lived with my grandparents in a white and brick rancher on the corner, directly across the street from Somerdale police station. My Poppy built our home with his own two hands; making it was extra special to me. He was a great construction worker and my Grammy was a cashier.

Daisy was a baby herself, just a teen. She spent most of her time hanging out with friends and working at the deli in a local Wawa, a convenience store. She knew I was being cared for when she was out.

Naturally, I don't have a lot of memories of her from this time. Fondly, I recall the smell of leather and vanilla musk and taking rides in her 1970s yellow Volkswagen Buggie. I spent most of my days with my grandparents. It left me craving the affection she could not express.

Grammy and Poppy were a huge part of my life. Thomas and Jane were highschool sweethearts. They truly were soul mates. Tom was rebellious for his time. Often, he was spotted sporting a pink Cadillac with matching attire.

Jane was gorgeous. She had exquisite hazel eyes and a heart-melting smile. They were always together, and when they were of age Tom proposed to Jane.

However, Thomas was Catholic, and Jane was raised Protestant and marrying outside of your religion was taboo. For this reason Nanny, Poppy's mom, forbade the union.

Nanny was a faithful woman and active in her church. Although she was fond of Jane, to her, the sacrament of matrimony was holy. They weren't allowed to be married in the church. Unfortunately, the union wasn't observed and therefore, they would be considered to be living in sin. Nanny wouldn't stand for this in her family. The couple didn't agree with her conviction, but honored her wishes to not marry. Times were very different then.

This decision devastated Jane. Knowing that she couldn't be with her one and only true love, she moved on. She and the next person she dated became good friends, and when he asked for her hand in marriage, she quickly accepted. She cared about John, but no one would ever replace Tom.

Her new husband was a veteran of World War II which added an interesting twist to their budding relationship. Not long after they wed, she gave birth to a little boy.

The circumstances and situations that our servicemen were enmeshed in were utterly disturbing to say to it lightly. He, like most of the military, suffered from Post Traumatic Stress Disorder, or PTSD. Back then, it was taught that "real men" don't ask for help, so therapy was looked down upon. Alcoholism was a common way to self-medicate, so when he became mentally and verbally abusive. After a time, she divorced him, although being a single mother wasn't acceptable in those days.

Tom enlisted in the army during the war as a radio control man. He missed Jane greatly. On his leaves he would sneak off and visit her. Their love was undeniable. Remembering that his mother forbade the idea of marrying outside of their religion, Jane knew what she had to do.

While Tom was away, Jane went to the local catholic church where she attended Catechism classes and got baptized into the faith, which enabled her to receive the sacraments including matrimony. Immediately after Tom completed his active duty, he declined reenlistment, and they wed.

Tom built a home for them across the street from my Ne Ne, his sister's house. Nanny lived there as well. He was always a family man and wanted everyone to be close. They had three children; including Johnny this made four. Two boys and two girls. They were thrilled with the life they finally got to create for themselves.

When I think of true love, I think of them. They are my true inspiration for a successful marriage. They became an image of happily ever after to me. My only hope of one day having my own.

Daisy, my mother, was their youngest child, and I was their first grandchild. Essentially, this makes me their baby's baby. I was the apple of their eye and was spoiled. The three of us were always together.

Every night after they got home from work, Grammy would prepare a home cooked meal. We would converse about the day we had after dinner, then Grammy and I usually played cards or any kind of game. We would then go into the living room and watch the nightly news. I would climb into Poppy's oversized brown armchair and snuggle him until I fell asleep.

Our holidays were like you would see on a television ad. Poppy built a huge platform around the Christmas trees. He set up a whole little city with collector mini trains. Grammy always adored shopping for others; She spared no expense especially for the holidays. When wrapping everyone's gifts, she made sure the tissue paper, ribbons and bows all coordinated, precisely lining up the paper edges so the patterns would perfectly match. Family traveled from other states to be together for dinner. Everyone arrived prepared with their favorite dishes. How I yearn for those days.

Every summer we would go to the campground for two to three months. We had a trailer at Lake Laurie. It was settled back in the woods in Cape May. I can still smell the mothballs and campfire as I reminisce.

We would go out on Poppy's boat, "The Janabelle Pearl'", named after Grammy. Bringing home freshly caught flounder for dinner was common and wonderful. When it rained, we would shelter inside and Grammy and I would play Kismet and cards. I was probably one of the best four-year-old poker players out there. She enjoyed gambling and she loved taking me to bingo at the hall with her.

After the rain stopped, Poppy would take me for walks so we could jump in the puddles. I thought it was our little secret. Poppy often had to leave the campsite and go home during most weeks for work. On these days, Grammy and I enjoyed spending our days at the beach and nights walking the boardwalk. Sometimes we would go to Cape May's large mini-mall filled with specialty stores. Other times, folks could find us at yard sales or out antiquing. We dined out a great deal since it was just the two of us. She always read my favorite books to me and sang nursery rhymes until I fell asleep.

It was more than a blessing to have my grandparents to care for me. When I was with them, I felt like a real life princess. They fashioned me in fancy dresses. My hair was long and light brown with loose curls and normally pulled up in pigtail. I loved to perform, and I enjoyed putting on plays for the adults. I felt like I could do and be anything I wanted.

Every summer, Cape May held a Little Miss Pageant. We watched it every year.

When I was five, I asked to be entered. Acting was my genuine passion, and I hoped this could get me in the door. My grandparents put me in my pastel rainbow checkered dress. It was my favorite. My hair was made up perfectly. We left it down with long finger curls. I was so excited. When we arrived not only did I not win; They did not even choose me to be a contestant. My little heart broke. Regrettably, this would be the one and only attempt in my life to be center stage. As minute as this sounds, this day had a lasting impact on my life.

Nanny was my best friend. She would watch me at her house while everyone was at work. She was always busy cleaning. Nanny even once bleached the family's toy poodle, Féfé, because his fur was yellowing. She loved cooking from scratch and over fed all of her guests. She never wanted to sit down because idle hands are a devil's plaything.

When she did, she would reminisce about her childhood in Philadelphia in the early 1900s. I always loved her stories and pleaded with her to tell me more. I would cuddle her and play with the flab on her aged arms. She remained devoted to her church and could travel all around the world on trips with other members. Like my grandparents, Nanny adored me and wanted the best for me. So much so that she paid for eight years of catholic schooling out of her social security check. It was absolutely what she considered the best and proper education for me.

While Nanny was busy preparing for dinner or occupied with her other daily duties, Ne Ne would often take me out shopping or we would go see a movie. Her daughter worked at the theater so we went quite often. It was always chilly there so she brought us homemade afghans to get cozy. We caught all the family friendly new releases. "The Muppets" were a favorite of ours. She loved the color purple. Almost everything she owned was this color and probably the reason it is my favorite as well. Even though my family structure was not like everyone else's', I know I was adored.

I was an affectionate child. I was a joyful and playful, and ultrasensitive child. I sensed the emotions of others and the natural environment around me. One day, I stumbled across a dead robin in our yard. It deeply disturbed me that not only had it perished, but was also alone. I felt it deserved a proper burial, so I set up chairs and an altar. I invited the neighbors. The memorial speech I gave was from the point of view of the family. I even took up a collection and buried the bird. Looking back, it's surprising how many adults showed up for a wild bird's send off.

Temper tantrums were commonplace when things didn't go how my little brain thought things were supposed to be. No one understood I wanted a "normal" family, so screaming it from the top of my lungs was all I knew to do. I was too young to articulate my feelings into words and being sensitive was hard for me. If anyone else was upset, I became upset. No one really knew what to do to help me. I would cry, I would kick my feet, I'd bang my head. I didn't fit inside the box of how children were supposed to behave.

The only reaction I received was to be sent to my room where my outburst only continued until eventually I would fall asleep. I could hear the adults teasing, saying that I was crazy. I was often questioned "what's wrong with you?" How was I supposed to know? I didn't understand myself. I wished I could give them an answer. I would get so worked up that I couldn't remember why I was mad. I tried to calm down but couldn't. The grown ups kept saying I was crazy, and I believed they might be right– that there was something wrong with me.

I'm grateful for my grandparents as they showed what a normal family should look like. Both parents were present. We would sit down for dinners together. We would go to the movies. There would be rules. We laughed and talked. Although I loved my grandparents very much, I craved that kind of relationship with my parents.

When I was four years old, Daisy started dating an incredible man named Johnny. They eventually got an apartment, and I moved in with them. He accepted me as his own. We had a natural bond. I even got another set of grandparents,Pop Pop and Nana, who treated me as they did their own blood. Wow, I was finally getting the family I always wanted.

Johnny started a towing company and they got married. Three years later they had my beautiful baby sister, who they named April. She was perfect, and I was so excited to be a big sister. I loved her to death, and I noticed a change with how Johnny paid attention to me, or at least I thought I did.

Now that Johnny had his own baby, I felt second best. There wasn't anything said to make me feel this way. Maybe I was jealous. The adoration I saw in his eyes for her said more than words. She looked like an actual little angel with her blond hair and blue eyes. I no longer remembered who my dad was, I knew it wasn't Johnny. No one had heard from Ricky in a few years; If they had they did not make me aware of it. I could see the difference between our relationship and the one he had with my sister. I was a child who wanted more than anything to have a normal family, and at that point I just felt like I didn't belong.

One day the family was getting all dressed up; I couldn't have imagined it would be one of the worst days of my life. I thought we were going to go to a party. My mom came in, placed a gold cross necklace in my hand, and then sat down on my bed and cried.

My Mom explained, "Poppy had been using the snow blower and had a massive heartache and passed away." I could not speak. I crawled under my bed and cried. I remembered the robin and knew I would never see him again. My mom later told me that was one of the hardest conversations she ever had to have.

I had never thought about people dying before; I suppose I had no reason. But by the tender age of six, I was questioning the purpose of life. Why were we here if we could be gone so quickly? What actually happens to you when you die? None of it made any sense to me. I was almost obsessed with it. My infatuation with death scared my grammy.

Poppy's passing hit me hard. They say a female's self identity of beauty comes from her father. This is what he always was for me. The only man who remained consistent in my life and he was gone. Still today I tear up thinking about him. I wish I knew him as an adult.

Grammy fell apart for a long time. She never really stopped missing him. She actually apologized to me after he died because it took her a long time to be around me. Every time she saw me she thought about him and it just hurt too much.

It's never actually been said but I believe this event was super hard on Daisy as well. Not too long after Poppy died, she and Johnny started fighting. She still wanted to party. She had just lost her dad and most of her teenage years were spent trying to raise me. Johnny was more stable, and they just didn't want the same things out of life anymore. They separated, and we moved back to my grandmother's. Grammy moved out and got a place with her sister but still assisted with the bills so we could get back on our feet.

Johnny being the honorable man that he is still took me for weekend visits. He really tried for me to keep my sister in my life. After years of me making mistakes, he could only see my mom when he looked at me and he told me as much whenever I messed up. No one could ever truly know how many times I have heard, "You are just like your mother." Nor could they understand the impact it had on me. I started feeling like I reflected other people's pain, and not understanding what this meant.

A few years later, we got a phone call on Christmas Eve.

My mom answered the phone. I heard her say "Yes, hold on."

She smiled and said, "Kris come here. Someone wants to talk to you."

I grabbed the phone and said, "Hi?" A man's voice spoke on the other end.

"Do you remember me?" The stranger questioned. I remained quiet as I searched my twelve-year-old mind for an answer. "It's your dad, Ricky," he continued.

My heart began beating with excitement, my eyes teared up but my voice was with no words.

"How have you been, kid?"

I mustered up some courage. "I'm good. Where have you been?"

The stranger replied. "Well...I live in Los Angeles, California. Sorry, it's been so long."

"What happened? Like why haven't you called or came to see me?" I questioned.

I suppose he wasn't expecting a series of inquiries right away.

There was a long pause before he answered.

"I was not allowed to see you and so when I moved to Las Vegas. I met a lady out there and I married her. She wasn't a good person. We were both on drugs. She stole everything I had; even your baby pictures. Then, I did something that wasn't so good either. I was broke. I robbed a liquor store. So, then I went to jail for five years. I'm doing much better now. I want to get to know you."

I started bawling.

"That's all I ever wanted! Do I have any brothers or sisters from you?" I asked.

He laughed and said "Not that I know of. I'll be in New Jersey next month and I was wondering if you would like to go out on a big fishing boat with me?"

"I would love to," I answered with passion

"Ok, kid, then it's a plan." He ended the conversation.

Once released he remained clean, and was going to college to be a drug and alcohol rehabilitation counselor. What a turnaround. I was so proud.

For the next few years he would make trips home to Jersey. It turned out he was gay. He struggled with his sexuality during his life and was now in a place where he felt he could be himself. He settled down with an older gentleman named Howard. I didn't care at all about his past, just what this could imply for us.

While this was an exciting time in my life, getting to know my dad for the first time, I was also struggling with my generational religious beliefs. All my classmates were excitedly preparing to get confirmed. In the Catholic church you are supposed to receive the sacrament of confirmation which is like baptism but now you're at an age to dedicate yourself. I don't see how in the eighth grade you are old enough to make this decision.

This usually entails a party and gifts afterwards. I knew how much this meant to my Nanny but something didn't sit right with me. They had exposed me to other religions, and I wasn't really buying into some traditions. So, I went to my teacher and requested to talk to a priest.

He met with me on a couple occasions. He appeared to be bothered by my insubordination.

I asked, "Can you please show me in the Bible where it says we have to go to Confession."

He said, "It is not in there. It is a tradition carried down; it is one of God's holy sacraments."

I thought it was arrogant that priests say they become God within the booth. I showed him where it clearly states Jesus had brothers and sisters. He then informed me by saying, "It is meant spiritually, not biological."

I also wanted to know why we pray to saints just as much as our father himself. None of it made any sense to me and the priest was more aggravated than helpful. The only thing he was helpful about was making my decision not to be confirmed catholic. After all, I felt it was his job to help the members of the church grow in their relationship with God.

I refused this sacrament. I didn't want to make that commitment although I knew it was breaking my best friend's heart because Nanny had paid for my schooling for all those years with dreams of attending my confirmation.

CHAPTER 1.2 TEENAGE YEARS

Puberty is hard on everyone. Unexplainable feelings and many bodily changes. It affected me more intensely than most of my friends. Premenstrual times often included suicidal ideations and even a few attempts.

For reasons that I only understand to be financial, they no longer could afford for me to attend Catholic school. I was switched to public school. The move allowed for a lot more freedom than I had been prepared for. I met a whole new group of people who introduced me to smoking cigarettes and began experimenting with alcohol and weed. Before, doctors medicated me, I medicated myself. As an adult, that's not a good idea, so imagine the decisions I made as a teen.

Now, if things lined up just right (well horrible wrong) and I drank when I was hormonal, it was a catastrophe. I was hospitalized with alcohol poisoning or for suicide attempts. I had a few run-ins with the police. Drinking made it easy for me to express how upset I was about everything in my life. Sadly, most of the time, my anger was directed at my mom for her inability to physically or emotionally show me love.

Of course, she took me to the doctor and explained that something had to be hormonally wrong with me. She had noticed my suicide attempts always occurred within a few days of my menses. They never even bothered to give me a blood test and referred me to a children's psychiatrist. Claiming it must be psychological and not physiological. Maybe that blood test would've made a difference in my treatment. I guess we'll never know.

I attended therapy regularly, but the doctor preferred to medicate me, which didn't work. I hated taking medicine, especially because this was only occurring one week out of the month but I was sedated daily as they tried to get it right.

I put myself in many possibly dangerous situations, but I wasn't always such a disaster. There were a lot of different circles of friends. I was still my fun playful and sometimes daring self. I loved everyone and did anything I could to help anyone in need. People that weren't in the best situation seemed to be attracted to me. I even convinced my mom to take custody of two of my friends that could no longer live in their home. I loved and cared for the needs of everyone but myself.

A new kid in town's father, Jurassic Joe, bought liquor for me and my friends for hanging out. At least that's what we thought. That was the innocence of a mind that hadn't been brought up around people who thought it okay to trick teenagers into being harmed.

One night, Jurassic Joe decided that being his company wasn't enough. I was very intoxicated that night, so I only recall pieces of the attack. He held me down. I was scared. I know I scratched his son's legs hoping they would make him stop. The kids stood to the side of me. One to the left and one to the right of the lawn chair I was in.

He did this in the side yard of his mother's house in front of his two sons. I suppose he was teaching them to be men. He didn't take my virginity, but he took my innocence.

I went home and spent close to a week in the tub trying to clean the filthiness off me. It didn't work. I couldn't stop feeling dirty. I was fifteen, and he was somewhere in his middle forties. I knew what he did was wrong, but I didn't know if I was raped. Society teaches us that if we act or dress a certain way, it's a woman's fault when something like this happens. I was wearing jeans with a tight striped shirt. I dressed like this all the time. It seemed appropriate to me however wasn't inside of this guy's brain.

I really had no business drinking, let alone with adults. I didn't want to say anything about what happened, so I eventually gave in and told my mom. She immediately went across the street to the police station and reported the attack. The on-duty officer ran his name and found out he had just been released from jail for statutory rape and was still on parole.

Boy, did this all cause an enormous problem with my neighborhood friends. Some stood by my side. The rest said I was just a drunken whore, and I deserved whatever *really* happened. I understood the boys' pain even then because they were only nine and fourteen years old. They witnessed the entire event. The police asked them to show them with dolls what they saw. Not to mention, they lost their dad again.

This event definitely affected my sense of self. On one hand, a much older man sexually abused me. On the other hand, I felt that two children were again left fatherless because of me.

Three years of high school, three different high schools and I was just starting my junior year.

I didn't like the first one. I had become accustomed to small classes with a lot of rules. The sizable crowds intimidated me. I went to a trade school instead. However, during that time I had gotten my stomach pumped again and a friend of mine shared this with the school. I had gotten alcohol poisoning. She went around telling everyone I was an alcoholic. This wasn't true. I didn't drink all that often but when I did I drank to get drunk. I obviously didn't know when to stop, but sometimes that was the point–I didn't want to.

The next day at school, I questioned my so-called friend about the rumors being spread as she was the only one who knew about my trip to the hospital. She didn't deny what she said. Before I thought twice about it, I grabbed her hair and pulled her backward. She was a lot bigger than I was, but in my rage I took her down with little effort.

Right before I swung, a teacher saw that I was about to hit her and quickly ended it. The girl who I thought I could trust my secrets with went to the assistant principal. "She was scared for her life" is what she told him. I was sent to a child study to be evaluated and was found to be a danger to myself and others. I was put on homebound for the rest of the year. This was a big deal. The boys were always getting in fist fights and never expelled over it.

They referred me to an alternative school, There was one problem– Most of them were all boys' schools. I was troubled, but intelligent, so I didn't fit the academic criteria for special education.

I was sent to the Therapeutic Learning Center. The bus ride took two and a half hours. I didn't mind because I was determined to graduate. I would do whatever as long as I didn't end up like my mom which was what everyone said would happen. I had two goals; no teenage pregnancy nor dropping out of high school. I assumed that's what everyone meant when they told me I would turn out just like her. Looking back, I don't think that she was so terrible, just immature.

I loved it there. Group therapy happened every day and one-on-one sessions were every week or more often if needed. I was really succeeding here. I held a 3.8 GPA. They hired special teachers for my more advanced classes. I started a yearbook for the school. I planned the school dances. One of their aids helped me get a poem published.

I talked them into holding a graduation ceremony for our class of five. I flourished in ways I wouldn't have in the other schools.

A lot of the kids were medicated with Riddelin and Adderall for Attention Deficit Hyperactivity Disorder, ADHD, They didn't enjoy taking their medicine either and then they would give it to me. My bus aide, who turned out to be a drug dealer, would bring me a free, small bag of coke every morning to get my day going. I later discovered he was attracted to me and thought that giving me free drugs would lead to getting into my pants.

I had already learned this lesson about being with older men who give these kinds of gifts and I never allowed myself to be alone with him. Sadly, all I had to do to get high for free was show up for the school. The uppers really helped me concentrate and get all my work done and may even have been attributed to me completing high school. I was never assessed, but looking back I may have had undiagnosed ADHD and needed what the other kids didn't.

Mom started seeing a man named Georgie for a few years prior. He thought of himself as a forever bachelor. He was a fun, genuine man who I grew to love very much. He never wanted kids of his own but life had a different plan for him.

When I was sixteen, my mom had my little brother Thomas; he was named after my Poppy. Then two years later, the night before my high school graduation, my twin brother and sister, Austin and Briana, were born. My family grew quickly. It was great to have little ones around. Unfortunately, Georgie suffered from cancer and died. My siblings were all under the age of five and had lost their father. I understood how unfair this was; My dad had been out of my life around the same age. They'd never have the chance to see their father again. I think this is where I was lucky. My dad and I could reconnect.

CHAPTER 1.3 EARLY ADULTHOOD

By age eighteen, I had graduated high school and was working in a Heritage convenience store. My best friend, Cassidy, had gotten me the job, and I was in a pretty balanced mental state. Cassidy started dating a guy from Camden, a rough city in South Jersey. She invited me on a blind double date to the movies with one of his friends.

On first appearance, I found Eli to be a handsome man. He was tall. He had a darker complexion of Spanish descent and had the prettiest dark brown eyes. However my approval was quickly shattered when he opened his mouth. First thing he said in a joking manner was "You're paying right?" Teasing or not I found this very distasteful.

The rest of the night was fun after learning to adjust my preferences to his humor. We began seeing each other on the weekly basis. Within the first six months, Eli and I ended up getting an apartment.

We had a lot of fun together. Eli and I both enjoyed video games and stand up comedy. My family really took a liking to him, especially Johnny and his parents. The apartment was walking distances to both of their houses. If we were not at home or work you would find us visiting with them.

Nana and I bonded over our favorite 8 O'Clock coffee. She always had fresh chocolate chip cookies waiting for us. If we caught her by surprise she quickly whipped up a batch. I enjoyed my time truly getting to know her. She was a fabulous mother of 8 and I learned alot from her.

Eli and I both worked at Jiffy Lube changing oil which oddly was one of my favorite jobs. We did well at situating our finances and everything seemed just right.

It had been about a year since we were together, and that Christmas Eli proposed to me. I excitedly said yes. We took on a second job delivering newspapers before work to help with the extra expense of a wedding. For the next couple months we began planning like crazy. I wanted everything to be perfect. And it was.

We were married outdoors on an older stage complete with stadium type benches. My stepdad, Johnny, had the reception at a fire hall that Pop Pop worked for. There was a DJ, a full buffet, and an open bar for our guests.

Although Ricky surprised me and attended, I asked Johnny to give me away. After all it was Johnny who raised me. That was not an easy task. He truly deserved the honor as a sign of gratitude. He was thrilled to do so. I felt a little guilty about not asking Ricky but Johnny's excitement reassured me that I made the right decision.

During the reception, Jess, one of my bridesmaids pulled me aside and shared something Nanny said that shook me to my core.

"Nanny told me there is a proverb; happy is the wife that the sun shines down upon," Jess said. "The sun came out right as you were saying your vows. Now, she can die at peace knowing you're ok."

Nanny was eighty-eight years old and had certainly lived a long good life, but that was beside the point. I instantly went into hysterics at the thought of losing her. I don't know why she felt it necessary to tell me this and especially at that moment. My life without Nanny has always been one of my greatest fears. I always said I was going to be put in a rubber room when this happened. I couldn't fathom that there'd ever be a day without her.

Reassuring myself that Nanny was fine at this present moment, I shook off the terrible thought to the best of my ability and tried to enjoy the rest of our night. I left to explore the east coast for the next two weeks on our honeymoon without a worry in the world.

Eli and I returned from our adventure and asked my mom if we could stay there while we built our credit and saved money to buy our own home. Of course she agreed. We knew it would be impossible to get enough money for a down payment and pay bills.

During this time, Nanny was hospitalized. I don't like visiting hospitals. There were two things Nanny always said– "I don't want to die alone" and "I don't want to die in a hospital." I still didn't go. I knew it was selfish, but ever since I lost my Poppy, I couldn't handle anything having to deal with death or dying.

I went to sleep and had a horrible dream. Nanny's heart monitor was flatlining when I saw it. At 12:58 am, I woke up in a state of fear. I couldn't breathe. I couldn't see straight and my heart was going a million miles a minute. It felt too real. I had convinced myself it was only a dream. I put on a familiar Disney movie and eventually fell back to sleep.

I slept in a little later than normal the next morning since I had been up half the night.

I made my way to the kitchen to make a pot of coffee, but my mom was already there.

"We need to talk," my mom said. Her face confirmed what I didn't want to be true.

My thoughts immediately raced to last night's dream. "Nanny died, didn't she?"

Mom quickly replied, "Yes at 1:03 am last night. I'm so sorry."

"No, it was 12:58am," I challenged. "I saw it happen." I explained the dream to my mom.

Our family had always been spiritually inclined so she wasn't nearly as horrified as I was.

How could this happen? I recalled her words–"I don't want to die alone." I concluded she didn't want to go alone, so I was there with her in the only way I could handle being with her. Maybe it was her way of preparing me as well.

Whatever it was, it scared me. This may have been the first experience where I thought I might be psychic. But my Catholic upbringing taught me that physics, mediums get those particular gifts from evil sources. So, does this mean that I'm evil?

Evil or not, I didn't like it. I struggled to sleep as fear gripped me from the idea that I saw exactly when Nanny left this earthly realm. Debilitating panic attacks weren't far behind as I was afraid I would have another "death dream" as I called them. Grammy took me to her doctor, and they prescribed me Xanax. One more drug to add to my growingly long list of medicine that merely kept me numb.

I couldn't feel.

I didn't feel fear nor anxiety.

I also didn't feel joy or excitement.

Even though Eli and I worked hard to save money and get our credit in order, we still could not get approved for a mortgage. We moved out of my mom's house and into a different apartment. And what was our next decision? It was time to have a baby.

I was twenty-two and most of my friends had kids and they seemed happy. Maybe this would be the solution for me to find the happiness that seemed so elusive. After several months of trying, we decided it was time to see a doctor. It had been two and a half years of not using protection and still no baby.

The doctor screened both of us. After being on the Depo shot for five years, I wasn't ovulating. I'd always been pretty safe because I didn't want to be an unwed mother. Eli also had a bigger problem. His swimmies were not swimming. We could fix my problem with a pill. He would need surgery.

We both desperately wanted to start a family, and we refused to let a few varicose veins get in the way. Eli set up an appointment to have them removed. We waited a few months for the results to come back so they could track the progress. In the first visit, the doctors performed the count, and we were told the unimaginable–Eli could never father a child.

We were shattered. We researched adoption and quickly found out we were too young and didn't make enough money for that process. We looked into invitro-fertilization using donor sperm. It was ten-thousand dollars per implantation cycle with only a ten percent success rate. Meaning, that if it didn't work the first time, you had to pay each time until it did. This simply wasn't feasible.

Think about the song by the female rock group, Heart, All I Want To Do Is Make Love To You, the part when the one nightstand sees her baby with his eyes. Well, I didn't want to pick up a random guy from a bar and hope to get pregnant. If Eli couldn't get me pregnant, we wanted it to be someone we knew. So, we asked a mutual friend that I knew from my neighborhood, Derrick.

Derrick had just been released from juvie and had told me he just had a baby. He agreed instantly, which I found a little strange. Such a big decision should have taken more time to make. However, Eli and I really wanted a family, so I went back on my fertility medicine and began tracking my ovulation to know for sure when was the correct time to be with Derrick. It was a success the first try.

I'm not sure that getting what you want at any cost is a good idea, but I know starting our family this way probably wasn't the best way to go about it. My marriage was never the same. Intimacy between my husband and I became strained. I know what I did, however; I felt as though it was mutually agreed upon and therefore justified. Eli started seeing a girl from his job when his manly instinct kicked in and he wanted to get even. I was scared about having a baby without a father so moving back to my mom's seemed like a good idea while I tried to work on what my next steps would be.

One night, Eli and Derrick both showed up on my mom's door-step. Eli was visibly distraught. He told me he had been hanging out in his old neighborhood again. He got scammed in a pool bet at one of the local bars and owed a thousand dollars to a gang member.

Somehow in the search for solutions to this problem, they came up with a "brilliant" idea to hold up a gas station.

I didn't want any parts of this plan. I argued with them both. The baby won't have a father if they do that. I've made mistakes, but I wasn't that stupid and I was pregnant. I had my baby to think about.

"I'm missing the respect I get in jail," Derrick said as he left.

"Bye," I said. "I'll see you in 5-10 years."

Derrick returned an hour later in a panic and had changed his clothes. The way the story was told was that Eli distracted one at-tendant by asking for help at the pump while Derrick pulled a knife, demanding money from the cashier. I listened to his account of what happened and they really believed they could pull off this heist.

I phoned my mom and told her not to come back to the house for fear that the cops would most likely be coming there. She thought it was just another one of my normal fits and insisted she had to put the kids to bed. I tried to explain what had happened, but that didn't deter her. I mean, it was her home, so I understood her not listening to what I was trying to tell her. I left and went to my old apartment.

While I was gone, Derrick returned to my mom's house in order to get rid of any evidence.

I was later told by my mom that the police did in fact arrive and Derrick opened the door. He resembled the man who robbed the gas station. They asked for his Identification. My mom let them search the house, and they found the outfit the robber had been wearing.

Derrick was arrested and because of his past offenses I would not see him for another ten years. Upon questioning he quickly gave up Eli. They charged him with conspiracy. He had never been in trouble before so they released him until court.

This turn of events shook me, but I didn't want Eli out of my life. We worked on our marriage, as well as the court case. We had been expecting a lawsuit from a car accident and used that money to hire one of the best mafia lawyers we could find. They are the best money can buy.

Court proceedings were postponed until after I had the baby. On September 25, 2000 Haley Marie was born. This little one was healthy and beautiful. Now, I was blessed with a chance to be the mother I always wanted to have and they sentenced Eli to five years. The money from the lawsuit came in the nick of time. I paid for the lawyer then took the rest of the money and bought a used, but lovely Infiniti, and paid for a one-year lease at another apartment. The next three months were stressful, but Eli became eligible for intensive supervised parole in that time.

I was a first time mom and my husband was in jail. Child services paid me more visits than I cared to count and Derrick's mom found out my daughter was his daughter and she wanted custody. She thought if Derrick would be a father to Haley it would keep him out of trouble once he got home.

I was doing my best, but I was lonely, so I started dating a friend of the family. He and my uncle were pretty close and had invited him on a trip to the Florida Keys. He brought me along for fun. I also found out that he was an addict. This is when self medication took a whole new turn for me.

We were beach bums and having a glorious time when we got a call from Daisy that Grammy had fallen ill. She had several massive heart attacks and needed to have surgery.

I was told that she died several times during the procedure. The doctors kept bringing her back but she would flatline again. I knew she had found Poppy again and no matter what the doctors did she wouldn't leave him.This is the only way I found peace with her passing.

Eli came home and did everything required of him by the courts successfully for the next few years. He really was a great dad to Haley; I was just to the point of wanting to give up on life when my dad called and offered to buy the three of us tickets out to Los Angeles. Wow! I thought it was just the thing we needed to get our family back on track.

The flight was ten hours long including a layover in Vegas. My dad arranged for us to stay at a pleasant hotel for three weeks. It was across the street from "The Price is Right" game show studio. He took me to his office and showed us around. I was ecstatic. It was as if this chance balanced out all those years he was missing.

We strutted down the Hollywood Walk of Fame. Ricky took us to fancy restaurants, and he took us to Disney. It was just splendid. I actually hadn't spent a prolonged period around my dad since I was little. It was bittersweet. Even as a child, I knew I needed him and that he was a good man. Addictions and anger don't care that a little girl needed her dad. It felt good to have my dad back.

When people say that life can, and most likely will change at the drop of a dime, you never know how fast that is until it happens. We had been home for two weeks when we got a call from Howard, my dad's partner. Ricky had been hospitalized, and the doctors found a tumor on his brain. It was PML, Progressive Multifocal Leukoencephalitis brain cancer. I researched what this was, and it turned out you only get it if you have Human Immunodeficiency Virus (HIV).

I quickly called to check on him and he explained he got HIV back in the 1980s and has been living with it since. He was scared I wouldn't let him see the baby if I knew. I was more educated than that but I understood his perspective–people are cruel.

The time I had getting to know my father better was short; within a few months he was gone too. Again, my heart broke like it did when I was young, only I wasn't ever going to see him again. Everyone I loved died.

Life at home was getting worse too. My mental health was declining again. My mom moved to North Carolina with her boyfriend where he had family. My brother, Thomas, stayed with us. And to top it off, Eli started selling crack in our complex again. Whenever he felt as though money was getting tight he regressed to this source of income. He started back in his teenage years when he lived in Camden. I told him I had a problem with it. Not just because it was illegal, but he knew I had an addiction. None of that mattered. He did what he wanted.

I was a hot mess and Eli had an addiction to money so he worked over eighty hours a week for an HVAC company. He would then stay up all night So he could stay on schedule with the crackheads. He always went overboard, and we never spent time together. I struggled with keeping my thoughts straight and the idea of taking my life seemed better than taking another breath. Pills never worked, so I crashed my car into the brick apartment building where we lived. I wasn't going fast enough to do any actual damage to myself. I ended up back in the crazy hospital which is where I felt I belonged.

I was inpatient for about a week. When I got home, the apartment manager told me that the cops were going to raid our place. I took the drugs to the upstairs neighbor to flush it. She let me in, but she was super angry. Eli had been sneaking and dating her girlfriend. He even used the credit that we fixed and the money from all this overtime and drug sales to purchase a house for them. I was devastated. We had our problems, but this blindsided me.

I didn't bother to ask questions. I called Eli and told him I was taking the children to North Carolina. I picked them up from school and took that six-hour drive.

To my surprise, as soon as we got there I was pulled into the other room and greeted with the one drug I was trying to escape. I didn't want to take part in that lifestyle, but at this point I wanted to escape from my reality and the drugs were ready and available to help with that.

I was unaware of how bad the mental dependency on crack had gotten down there. I quickly learned what long-term drug use looked like and what it does. One thing–it's no respect for people. Just because you're a parent, just because you're a model employee, just because you live in a mansion, a drug habit will bring you down to the pits of hell if you let it.

My mom's boyfriend worked with this guy, Jerome, who had received a large financial settlement. My mom's boyfriend thought it would be a good idea to pimp me out to him so we could continue to get high. Jerome was sixteen years older than I was. Maybe he thought better of me than to do what my mom's boyfriend wanted. He asked me to come and be with him after learning of this plan. It wasn't necessarily a better choice as he was also an addict and without a permanent address.

He had been house hopping, sheltering where he could, so he got a hotel room for us. This would be our home for about six months. I had gained over thirty pounds and missed my last five cycles. I took multiple pregnancy tests, each one came back negative.

I found a local gynecologist who gave me a blood test which verified the same results I had received. Perplexed, the doctor sent me for an ultrasound.

During an ultrasound looking for tumors in my belly they found a six-month-old baby. This would be baby number twenty for Jerome, something I only found out after revealing that I was expecting. He seemed thrilled over the idea of another. Little did I realize after twenty children a parent in North Carolina is no longer responsible to pay any child support.

I didn't want to raise my family in a hotel, no matter what my struggles were so we moved into a townhouse.

Even with the baby on the way, Jerome didn't want to stop getting high. I didn't want to hurt the baby, and I worked hard to not answer the cravings of my addiction. This became a problem between us. I suppose when you already have twenty kids that you're barely caring for (if at all), the well-being of the next one isn't much of a priority.

One night, Jerome stole my car to go to a party. He returned the next morning, and I argued with him about leaving me and Haley without transportation. Before I saw it coming, he backhanded nearly knocking me to the floor. I grabbed Haley, ran to the car, and drove straight to my mom's. To my disappointment, they did not welcome us this time. Her boyfriend said there wasn't enough room there for me, especially since I was expecting another.

Out of desperation, I called my dad's sister, Kathleen. I had seen them through the years but truly didn't know them. It surprised me that she agreed because it had been a long time since I was in touch. So, at six months along with a six-year-old in tow, we took a twelve hour bus trip from North Carolina to New Jersey on a Greyhound carrying all of our belongings. This wasn't a minor feat. When I arrived at my aunt's house, I was just thankful to have somewhere to stay.

She was strict, and I thought it was unnecessary. I was an adult with my child. Once you become an addict, you are not viewed the same ever again. I worked hard to keep her place clean–they used me as a live-in housekeeper and babysitter for my stay. There were no boundaries to what I asked of me, even having me stain the hardwood floors of the house, and at the time I could hardly see my feet when I stood. I knew it wasn't healthy, but I didn't have anywhere else to go.

What I thought would be a peaceful and healthy experience turned out to be a burden to me and my daughter. To say that I was overwhelmed would be an understatement. I didn't grow up in this kind of family and did not know what the rules were to living like this.

I'm sure she was trying to teach me how to be responsible but it was too much and I wasn't in the headspace to receive the lessons. Haley wasn't happy, either so we left, staying from place to place until I had Trinity Jane. She was another absolutely perfect little girl, only now I believed I'd never be a fit mom. My mom was a better mother than I was and she was just a teen. What was my excuse? I loved my girls, but somehow wasn't able to be the mother they deserved.

My best childhood friend, Jess, took us in until I could get on my feet. I went to social service for help and got lucky–the housing list had opened up on the day I went into the office. This was a rare opportunity. The wait usually takes years and still not guaranteed a voucher for housing. All I had to do was get a job and find a place.

So, I did just that and I felt a little better about myself. Maybe I could do this alone. Cassidy helped me find used furniture and got some baby supplies for me. We had been friends since middle school so once she heard about my predicament she was right there for me.

I found a secretarial position in Cherry Hill. Great, right? Not so much. The only place I could find to take the housing voucher was in the next county in Williamstown. This meant taking three buses, leaving at four in the morning to get to work on time.

I quickly made friends with a neighbor and agreed to pay her to get Haley to school and watch Trinity. I did this for the first six months with success. However, almost every penny I brought home went to my neighbor, all except for the bus fare.

Thoughts of suicide crept up as the feeling of not having enough and not being a wonderful mom to my girls weighed me down. Haley's grandma, Mom Mom, questioned her non-stop about my personal affairs. She hated being asked and hated even more having to answer, but this time she was worried about me and told her what was going on at home. That's all she needed to hear and child protective services was at the house. I lived in a different county now so they were not aware of all the calls that mom Doris had placed on me before. That day the unthinkable happened–they took both of my kids. They were truly all I had, my family. I had nothing and no one. They might as well have killed me.

CHAPTER 1.4 THE DARK YEARS

My neighbor's kids and his friends were in their senior year of high school. They were all actively using heroin, a drug I had always been frightened of. I had seen them get high before. I thought, "what a mess" as they nodded off. The pain of my girls being taken wouldn't stop. I wanted to die and if I couldn't die, being numb was the next best thing. I had never used a needle before and it didn't matter.

Most people usually go from pills to snorting to shooting. Nope, I couldn't stand to be alive. I hoped this would take away this torture and that it did. The first time that needle was pushed into my vein everything immediately melted away. I was in love and no longer cared. All by myself in the world. I was no longer heart-broken from all the loss I had l survived. It was gone. All gone, at least for a few hours at a time.

Heroin–I found my new best friend. The one I had been looking for my whole life. It was the love I hadn't felt before. It was a way to escape the pain. I'd travel anywhere and do anything as long as I had it. Until a few months later the first time I couldn't get money. My new friend showed its ugly face as physical withdrawal.

I knew about addiction, but this was a whole different ball game. The sleepless nights, hot flashes, the chills, the body cramps, and the vomiting. During that time, they could find me sleeping in the bathtub. It was the only place I could feel any relief. It became a vicious cycle of hide and seek until my next fix.

I had become nothing more than a common junkie and I hated it. I thought about the reprehensible heartache I was causing my kids, the only people I really felt that still loved me in the world. How would they ever forgive me? How would I forgive myself?

I wanted my girls back. The only way I figured I could get them back was to tell child services about my habit and get some help. With no other good options, I was reluctant. I only cared about getting the kids back, but that call was going to give them a reason to find me inadequate. I was taught early on by mom that there are two things that were unacceptable: lying and stealing. I always lived by these values. I know that this call made things worse, but I had to take this chance to get my girls so we could be a family again.

Social workers quickly sent me to a methadone clinic, set me up for counseling, and parenting classes, allowing me two visits a month at the state building. I made every appointment, session, and visit. All of this on a bus. However, the methadone didn't help. It turns out when methadone, when combined with xanax along with all of my other psych meds it was just as bad as heroin. Basically, I was a zombie.

The Nazis created methadone. It was used to kill pain and keep the soldiers under control. I'd love to know why any doctor thinks that this would be okay to use on drug addicts. It was liquid handcuffs. Missing a dose was pure torment.

I played this game for a year and a half. I did everything that they requested. When I had my next court date, the judge was pleased and advised me I could get my kids back as long as I could exit the maintenance program. I accepted the challenge with the belief that doing so would show my kids that I still cared.

The typical protocol for weaning off of methadone is to decrease the amount given by 2 mg every 3 days. I was on 160 mg. I didn't have time for this. I requested to come down 10 mg a day for 2 weeks. I left the program with two weeks to spare in order to test clean for my upcoming court date.

I attempted to hide the circles under my eyes with cover up and disguise my anguish with a counterfeit smile . I arrived at the courthouse and tested clean. I kept my end of the bargain and a new dilemma had developed. Withdrawal from Methadone is incredibly harder than heroin. Heroin withdrawal usually lasts 5 days whereas methadone can take up to six months to come out of your system fully.

I was so worried about getting my girls back that I never considered that I would still be too sick to care for them.

Haley was old enough to get in the fridge and could entertain herself by watching the television, but Trinity was barely a toddler. She needed more care than I could give. Gratefully, my mom suggested she keep Trinity until I was feeling better. I informed my worker of the arrangement, and she agreed that taking advantage of the help would be good for me and Trinity. However, this ended up back at court. Trinity's foster family had heard that "their" child was in North Carolina with my mother and the judge felt as though I should spend the time bonding. She obviously didn't understand what happens during withdrawal. She immediately called my mother and gave her three days to bring Trinity back into the state's care or she'd be convicted of kidnapping. My mother brought her back, and the courts took my girls away again.

I was perplexed. How could my workers agree to the arrangements and the judge say we were doing something illegal? I was still having withdrawals, and some days were harder than others.

I was back to square one, and it wasn't fair. I was tired and had no fight left in me. So, what do people do when they don't know what else to do? They go back to what's familiar and as a junkie I was no different. This time around, I felt as though there was no end in sight. I couldn't find a reason. They took away the only reasons I had from me all while I tried to heal.

I could write a whole series of books about how many times I overdosed or the endless accounts of waking up with no recollection. I could share with you all the relationships I had where our only genuine bond was a needle. I could go over what it was like to sleep on sidewalks and in abandoned houses. As an occupation, I could talk about scrap metal and theft. I find no solace or purpose in doing that. I think it's important to only share experiences that permanently affected the person I'm Today. I'm not who I used to be.

Five years had passed in the blink of an eye, and they did not return my girls to me. The damage that had been caused to the kids became painfully clear. Children's services often called me to the psych ward for Haley. She started cutting herself. Trinity knew who I was but never had a chance to be very attached. I witnessed the cycle repeating in a full circle in real time. Knowing that I caused this to happen to my children made me sick to my stomach.

During one of my many trips to the endearing dumps of Camden, I stumbled across a fellow addict. He seemed safe enough, so I invited him back to my place for a shower and some food. I felt blessed to have a roof over my head after so many times not knowing where I was going to lay my head at night. I lived alone, but I didn't enjoy it. There was too much time to think. I allowed him to stay for a few weeks.

I got very ill. This wasn't dope sick. My skin radiated yellow, and I was extremely constipated. To get some relief I gave myself an enema. To my horror I only dispelled blood. I refused to go to a hospital because that meant withdrawal. A few days later, I went to my regularly scheduled doctor's appointment. I was off of the methadone and on Suboxone for maintenance. This medicine includes an opiate blocker hoping to deter addicts.

As soon as the doctor saw me, he called the hospital to admit me. It turns out that my new friend had passed me both Hepatitis B and C. That prize landed me in the hospital basement for the next month.

The court date was fast approaching for me to keep my visitation, and I was still in the hospital. I knew if I didn't appear in court I'd lose it all together. I signed myself out, and I called for a ride. The courthouse was only the next town over. However, I still wasn't well. We got lost and arrived an hour late. Once inside the courtroom, and in front of the judge I passed out, and an ambulance was called and they readmitted me. It didn't matter that I showed up; it didn't matter that I was sick. It was as if I hadn't shown up at all and my records indicated.

The courts didn't care, and I didn't bother to dispute. I worked up the will to fight for my girls and it was taken away again.

After so many years of Trinity being with the same family; I feared taking her back would cause more damage than good. The family that cared for her all these years truly loved her. They were financially stable and could provide ways for her I could never. It was the single hardest decision of my life however I agreed to sign the adoption papers and end this seven-year battle once and for all.

For another few weeks in the hospital I stayed asleep, only to awaken with a room full of medical students. I could hear the doctor reviewing my charts with them. She explained that with bilirubin levels so high my outcome would be terminal. This false information was expressed to the student doctors without fully reviewing my chart. I was only in there until the virus passed through my system. It must have given me my fight back. A week later I was given clearance to go home with follow-ups appointments and instructions to rest.

I did as I was told and went to my specialist. After doing some more blood work, he was in disbelief. He could see I had contact with these viruses however I had no viral load. This was a miracle.

Hepatitis C almost always needs a strict regimen that takes six months and I never had one started.

I had more loved ones on the other side than were left on the earthly plane. I truly believe they are always pulling strings for me. They even sent me a real life angel. His name is Bart. He has been beside me through this journey since I first arrived back in New Jersey.

Bart was in his seventies, thirty-two years older than I am. He is peculiar. Some would say he is eccentric. He is retired from American airlines where he worked as an airplane mechanic. He spends most of his days caring for me and his dogs. It was never a romantic relationship although there were a few people jealous of our friendship who implied otherwise.

He would ride his bike twenty miles at a time to help me meet my needs. He always made sure I was safe and fed. We took many expeditions by bike. He always directed me by saying, "You want to make a hard left at the stop sign." It always brought a smile to my face when he would gently hum "Dum Da Dum Dum" it meant he was having a good day. Many people couldn't handle him and would often say mean things. Not me. I always saw the beautiful heart he had. It made me oblivious to his flaws. I helped him a lot with technology or making phone calls. It became a mutually beneficial relationship. I was happy to help and wished I could do more.

It amazes me to have been so blessed. I knew fully that I didn't deserve his help. Yet he saw potential through all my faults and believed in me even when I didn't believe in myself. I will be forever grateful.

Haley was always running away from foster homes to come see me. I didn't discourage her from running away–it gave me more time to spend with her although our visitations were supposed to be supervised.

Haley visited my mom's house on the day that I was there. I knew her mental health wasn't getting any better; the scars on her arms and thighs made it very clear.

She pulled me into the bedroom.

"Mom, we need to talk," she said. Those words always make me nervous.

I replied, "Yea, Hal, what's up?"

"I have never felt like a girl," she explained. "Ever since I can remember I felt like I should have been born male."

I was pretty shocked. I knew she had different sexual orientations however this was brand new and I was very confused. How could a twelve-year-old possibly know this?

"Are you sure?" I asked. "Could this just be a phase?"

I spent most of her life envisioning her walking down the aisle and watching her give birth. All the things a mother and daughter bond over. This changed everything in my mind. I'd have to get to know a new person. I loved my child, and I mourned the loss of my daughter while learning to love and understand who I was going to know as my son. It was difficult, but I agreed with persuasion from the state,since she had been in their custody they had influence over this decision but still needed me to sign to allow my first-born to start hormone therapy. I didn't know if I had done anything to make the damage worse, but I never wanted to have to see my child with any new, self-inflicted cuts. If this was honestly how she felt I was going to stand behind him.

During the process, I definitely made mistakes. Pronouns were really hard for me to get used to. I would take longer than he wished to agree to important decisions and at age sixteen he legally changed his name to Isaac Mathieu.

A few years had passed, and nothing had changed. Until one day I was lying on the couch and I felt something move inside me. I calculated the days. I was four months late for my period but this wasn't uncommon for me. To be safe, I got a home pregnancy test. It was positive, so I scheduled an appointment with an OB/GYN for it to be confirmed.

I was nervous and had a nagging feeling that something was wrong. When I saw the doctor, I was honest from the door about my history of drug use and what medicines I was taking. He confirmed the pregnancy and checked over the baby and I thoroughly. We heard the baby's heartbeat, and he reassured me everything was fine. The doctor decided Subutex was the best option.

Subutex is another maintenance drug without the blocker. Getting pregnant while using causes the baby to be physically addicted to opiates as well. Stopping all opiates during pregnancy verifiably forces a miscarriage.

I had only been with one person during that time. He was more like a friend I bought drugs from. Occasionally we partied together but nothing serious.

I hesitantly notified the father. Just as I expected he was furious and as expected he told me to get an abortion. I knew he wouldn't be happy, but I didn't think he would want me to kill a five-month-old fetus. I don't have a judgment if someone decides that abortion is the route for them. Even though I had already lost two, I couldn't do it.

I began preparing for her arrival. I went shopping for all the supplies an infant would need. I went to my ultrasound appointment as scheduled. The tech measured her growth and checked to make sure her organs were forming correctly. The tech seemed eerily quiet; That's always a clue of some dark news to come. Something was off with one valve of her heart. They referred me to Children's Hospital of Philadelphia (CHOPS) for further testing. I called for an appointment but couldn't be seen for another month. As if my life wasn't stressful enough, this made my concerns worse.

While waiting for my appointment at CHOPS, I kept my regular checkups with follow up ultrasounds. The nurse set me up and started an ultrasound. She asked me to wait a minute and went and got the doctor. To their shock, she no longer had a heartbeat. I looked at the monitor, her lifeless body floating around inside me.

They quickly apologized for not listening to my concern and gave me two options. I could either immediately go to the hospital to be induced or call the abortion clinic which would allow me to be put to sleep and have her removed. I was twenty-seven weeks along.

I was too shocked to even think about this so I went home and talked to my mom. She called around to clinics for me but it was late in the day on a Friday and none of the clinics were available to schedule me. It was also the weekend after Trinity's birthday and for the first time in a long time; I was allowed a supervised visit with her.

I did my best to smile and make believe that everything was all right. The last thing I wanted to do was let her know that her baby sister had passed. She had enough loss and change in her young life. By Sunday I knew I was going to have to go to the hospital. The cramps were getting bad and the thought of carrying my dead baby haunted me.

We had to go to two hospitals that day. The first one refused to deliver the baby because there wasn't an on-site blood bank and this procedure could be dangerous. We arrived at the second hospital, and they immediately admitted me.

On May 6th, 2013, I was dilated and induced. My placenta had separated, and I pushed out a sack. The doctors carefully cut it open and removed my one pound baby girl.

They did what they could to make the pain of delivering her easier but there wasn't anything or no one that could do that. She was cleaned off and dressed. They made her a special gown out of a baby blanket because of her size. My mother and I held her for a few hours before we said goodbye and they took her to the morgue.

I already felt like a no-good piece of s*** because I failed my first two children. F*** life–that was my attitude, I felt as though I killed my baby. With the lifestyle I'd been living, for so many years, how could I not think that? The doctors disagreed and reassured me that there are plenty of women that have used drugs up to the full term of the pregnancy and still give birth to healthy babies. The maintenance medication shouldn't have done this. There was no changing my mind. All I could think about was how peaceful it would be to get one last and excellent shot and never wake up.

I didn't care anymore. Dying would've been kind as living was torture. Three years had gone by and no amount of drugs seemed to kill me. I may have gone unconscious or had seizures but I'd always wake up and start over again. I had no regard for the law and I was done with the hell I had created for myself. I'm not sure how I survived.

CHAPTER 1.5 SEEMINGLY UNFAVORABLE SAVING GRACE

Divine intervention comes in so many unexpected forms. What may look more like devastation and suffering could turn into a hugely unexpected, undeserved blessing.

On one of my many run-ins with the law, I was once again withdrawing from opiates and benzos. I dropped my boyfriend, Kaden, off at the hospital because he was having hallucinations associated with his withdrawals. To his good fortune, he was admitted and sedated, which was fabulous for him but ticked me off. I took his car and bought a half pint of rum. I never really enjoyed drinking since I was a teen. It caused many problems for me and that day would be no different. I just wanted the anxiety to go away.

While I was drinking, I got a phone call that someone had Klonopins. I went and picked up ten and took them.

I'm still not sure why, but I thought it'd be a good idea to go to an old friend of mine's house. Who was the manager of the apartment complex I lived in with Eli. I was hoping to find a place to live but was in no condition to ask.

I wasn't there for more than a few minutes when to my utter surprise, cops showed up. Apparently, a concerned citizen called about my erratic driving and called them.

What beautiful timing. The high from the pills that I had already ingested had kicked in. As the report said, I was visibly intoxicated. I had elbowed one cop while trying to make my escape. My memory of the event was blurred. Ultimately, I got what I definitely needed and some things I definitely didn't; They took me to the hospital for an evaluation, and was left with a ton of additional charges.

The psychiatric evaluation and observation gave me time to sober up. Well, making good decisions still wasn't something I practiced, and I called Eli to come and pick me up, at this point adding a charge of escape to my growing list of complaints. Eli and I had remained friends throughout the years.

I had been in and out of municipal trouble for some time and had grown quite accustomed to the process. They usually drop state charges back to municipal. This time my charges were in the Superior Court. I know I probably should've been worried, but considering the whole incident happened during a blackout, in my mind, it never happened. Eli dropped me off.

I reconnected with Kaden, a childhood friend. I had known since we were twelve. His family often took us to christian youth group at their church. For over twenty years he was one of my best friends. He always kind of had a thing for me but I was never attracted to him like that. We remained friends until my mid-twenties. Sadly, we lost contact when I moved to North Carolina.

Years later, Kaden found me online, and at the time we were both struggling to get off opiates. We erroneously thought we could help one another with this. We just fed each other's monkeys.

Kaden had always been supportive and caring towards me growing up. He would get in a fight with anyone that said or did anything to hurt me. After some time, he turned into the person who he once would have defended me from. Addiction changes the behaviors and personalities of even the best person. I should've left when I had to lie to everyone about the time he gave me a black eye.

How silly did I sound saying I had hit my face on the handlebars of my bike? Thinking back to it, I'm glad that no one questioned the answer I gave.

Many people wonder what makes anyone stay in an abusive situation. I can't answer for others, but I felt as though that I deserved to be abused. I didn't care for myself and it made sense that no one else did.

Kaden and I went to New York for rehab and there was a fire in the building during my stay. I saw this as a "sign" so we left. We were stuck living in NYC for a few days before we could get up enough money to get home. When we arrived back in Jersey, I went back to my mom's door. I stood on the porch for a moment before knocking. My mother's house was always somewhere I could go back to, but I guess after so many chances, my visits were becoming a pain.

My brother answered and wouldn't allow me in. In fact, he was so furious that I was there that he told me to never come back. He demanded that I never be around my family again. Kaden was allowed at his parents' as long as he wasn't with me. We both ended up staying in a house he used to own, but had been repossessed and had no electricity or running water. Addiction separates families, but someone has to protect the loved ones. I wondered if this is why my dad had to stay away when I was little. Was it the same as what I was going through?

After a few years of living in the only place, we could afford to live and still get high, we looked for places away from the city. My hope was if I made it harder for us to get to Camden, perhaps we could stop. We ended up renting a small room from an older couple who lived on the lake in Franklinville. It's further in the boonies than I had ever lived before. We didn't have a car to get back and forth to Camden after all. One thing addicts forget is that we bring ourselves wherever we go and how tenacious we can be when we need that fix.

In no time, I learned the five-mile route to the nearest bus stop. Then I'd take a nearly two-hour bus ride to get back to Camden. I did this dope sick. Depending on my finances, I'd do this several times a week, sometimes several times in a day. I repeated this cycle until one day I lost feeling on my left side.

I hesitated to call 911, but the situation made it necessary. When I arrived at the hospital, I found it peculiar that an officer stayed with me. I asked him what his deal was, and he informed me I had a felony and failure to appear charge. Once cleared, they had instructed him to take me to Camden County Correctional Facility.

I didn't have a physical address for so long and I had missed several court dates. I knew it was my responsibility to provide them with one, but I never had a steady one to give.

Jail provided me with a chance to detox during the thirty-day stay. I had one of the strictest judges the county offered. Judge Purple did not play. She took not showing for court as a personal disrespect. They released me with an ankle bracelet after much persuading.

Thirty days clean. This should've given me a fresh start being that I no longer had the physical illness. However, Kaden picked me up from jail, having already grabbed me a bag of our favorite poison and had it all set up. It was my welcome home gift. I was high before we drove out of the city.

Part of the agreement to be released was weekly check ins and drug testing. They had given me an 8pm curfew. I could never keep the curfew or pass the drug test. My officer was kind and was genuinely concerned with keeping me alive.

My ninety-day bracelet turned into six months because of many court continuations. Eventually, Judge Purple sentenced me to five years of probation. If I couldn't successfully complete this program, I was looking at ten years of incarceration in the state penitentiary.

She acknowledged I suffered from mental health issues and addiction. I was given a MICA, Mentally Ill Chemically Addicted specialized probation officer. I called him Mr. H. He and I would spend a lot of time together over the following years.

After many failed drug tests, they sent me to an eight hour a day outpatient rehabilitation. I still couldn't stop using. In time, I gave him no other option but to violate my probation.

Back to court. Even after skirting the rules and continuing to get high, I should've been taken straight to jail for a decade. As divine favor would have it, I was given a break and told I had to go to an inpatient facility. I was scared, but it was a month at New Hope, a rehab facility, or ten years some place worse. As part of the program I agreed to take the Vivitrol shot which prohibits the euphoria opiates produce.

In October 2015 while in New Hope something started clicking.

Upon release, I was ready to attempt living clean. I got back home where I found Eli with Kaden. Needles and other paraphernalia were all over my living room coffee table. I was furious. They were both very high, and both knew I was coming home. They knew the consequences if they found me getting high or being around people who were using. They were fully aware of what would happen. Addiction takes away the ability to care in any real way. This time was like all other times before with them. I guess they thought I'd join them.

I quickly gathered some of my belongings and went to stay at my mother's house. Although my brother wasn't thrilled by the idea, he knew I was trying to do better for myself. He agreed to give me another chance. The next morning Eli called me, sounding frantic. Kaden was seizing and unresponsive. When I arrived, the apartment was covered in blood. It was terrifying. I called 911.

Once doctors stabilized Kaden, he told me he had overdosed because I left him. Me, being the sucker that I was, tried to support him over the next few weeks he spent in the hospital. I now know that this is a technique narcissists will use to regain any amount of control they had in your life.

While he was in the hospital, I moved back into the apartment and started attending Narcotics Anonymous. I felt I didn't fit in. I allowed Kaden to come and live with me. He promised he would stay clean. I knew too well what it is like to be homeless and I hated being turned away from people I loved that I thought should've been willing to help me. This wasn't a smart idea.

Every addict turns to something else to replace the feeling that other drugs give, especially when we first try to quit. In most cases its excessive caffeine or nicotine. In his case it was alcohol. He had been at his boss's house drinking. I had been calling him a lot to make sure he didn't sneak off. This infuriated him. He came home but it would've been better if I let him stay where he was. It led to the worst beating I'd ever had.

When he arrived home, he began screaming at me. "Why won't you just let me stay out and have fun? I'm a grown man. I will do what I want from now on." Kaden flipped over the coffee table, tossing the chicken noodle star soup I was eating all over and embedding it in the carpet. The mess he just created made him even more angry at me.

"You stupid bitch!" Kaden exclaimed. "Look what you made me do!" He grabbed me by the neck, held my belly downwards. "Clean them up," he demanded. "I don't care if it's one tiny star at a time." Out of fear, I obeyed.

As I cleaned, he left the room and went to the bathroom. I saw this as my chance to make a beeline to the door. It was dead bolted, so I was frantically fumbling to get the locks undone until I heard the toilet flush and began banging on the door and started screaming. "Call the cops! PLEASE Call the cops!"

He drug me by my hair in the bedroom, threw me on the bed, and started strangling me.

"If I can't be with you, then know one can have you," Kaden exclaimed.

He continued screaming at me. "Your kid is mixed," he said with a chuckle "No other man in their right mind would date a junkie n@g**r lover, anyway."

Kaden's grip grew tighter as he hollered. "I'm gonna kill you this time. No one is coming to save you."

I eventually passed out. When I woke up, it was morning, and he had no memory of the night before.

I figured I was better off in jail than I was home. I tried to get high, but I was still on Vivitrol; It doesn't allow the sensation of being high even though it's very possible to overdose. You feel nothing except severe agitation over wanting something so bad at knowing it won't work. While trying to find something that would get me some kind of high, I found out that Vivitrol does not block the feeling of cocaine, so we did that only a few times.

Those few times were enough to violate my probation again; this wasn't necessarily my goal, but the nonsense I was doing had to serve a purpose. This time, Judge Purple had no mercy. I spent ninety days in the Second Chance Program inside the jail before she would even hear my case. During my time there, I had no choice but to explore my reasons behind using.

While on my one daily call with my mother I was told that Jess had been found dead in an abandoned apartment. The medical examiners estimated she had been deceased for two weeks prior to being found. The thought of my childhood best friend being gone and no one even bothering to find her made me realize how addicts are really looked down upon.

She had two children that were left motherless. I reflected on my own children and what it would do to them if it was me instead of her. It was just as likely, but I was spared. So I started opening up to people and made a few friends. It was nice to have people that I could relate to that also wanted to get better.

When the judge did finally hear my case, she read the review Ms. Marsha, the incredibly stern but genuinely caring counselor, had included. She saw the efforts I had made. Instead of reverting my sentence she allowed me to go to a halfway rehabilitation program. This is a long-term rehabilitation center that would attempt to teach me how to live as a functioning adult.

Officers cuffed and drove me an hour and half away to Absecon, which is near the Jersey shore. In this program facility more intensive therapy was employed. I literally had to be taught how to live again. From getting up and making my bed, to cooking for a group of thirty other women, and what was the hardest of all, to heal. They provided me with the skills to remain substance free and become a productive member of society.

For the first two months they made me to sit in silence for six hours a day. I had to read self-help books and reflect through writing–it felt like utter torture. Over time, it worked. It forced me to take responsibility for my actions and reconcile with myself and others. I had to get creative because it's hard to do this with others when it's only you there.

The last month I lived there, I was allowed to work part time. This permitted me to get reacquainted with society and to stay clean. They saw I could do this. They then sent me to an Oxford House, a ¾ house.

Staff do not run Oxford House's. It's a group of other same-sex people in recovery. You must hold a job, pass random drug tests, and attend meetings. I attended Genesis, an outpatient group based rehab,for three times weekly counseling. I became a server at Collingswood Diner. It was right outside of Camden, so I remained on the shot just in case I got a wild hair up my butt one day.

I discovered I really enjoyed being a waitress. I liked the fact that my services directly affected how much I would make per day. My favorite thing that it provided for the first time was independence.

It had been nearly a year since I had been clean so my mom and siblings allowed me to come stay with them. This was temporary until I decided where I wanted to live. My mother and brother were planning to move to Virginia in a few months so there wasn't a lot of time to do so.

My real journey was just beginning. I received a Facebook request from Jeremy, an acquaintance from my past. He was my neighbor's son in Stratford. There had been some mutual attraction about twenty years ago, however we were both in serious relationships. Aside from a little kiss, nothing was pursued.

Jeremy invited me on a date. I assumed it was for a fling. There were a few failed attempts. I'm unsure if it was the fact that he could not borrow a vehicle and was apprehensive to tell me he did not own his own or perhaps he was nervous. We had not seen one another in about ten years. Either way, he picked me up. We went out and enjoyed a meal at the diner and ended up at a cheap motel for the night. The next morning he brought me home, and I figured that would be that.

I had been working at the diner for about six months. I was killing it financially for the first time in my life. So when my family left for Virgina I was no longer fearful of being homeless. I had already saved a few thousand, and I knew I could easily afford to stay at a hotel near my job and to use a Lyft to work. I called Jeremy and asked if he could help move me in.

Being able to support myself made me happy. I spent most of my time at work. I was making friends, and I didn't use. Motel life was getting costly, so I started applying for places to live. With my background, it took many denials before they approved me for housing.

The location wasn't favorable. It was a trailer in the town next to Camden. Being out of other options, I knew I'd have to be extra vigilant. It wasn't too far from work. I was just grateful I was being offered a chance.

Now I'm always going to be an addict and no one is ever perfect. On occasions, Jeremy and I would partake in a few cocktails. At the trailer we were buzzed and arguing and I told him I thought I was pregnant. I wasn't late for my period yet so I'm not sure why I had that thought. We had only been seeing each other for two months and we were about to be forty so this was unlikely.

A few days later, I sent him a picture of my positive pregnancy test. We were both pretty surprised by this. He was in disbelief more than I was. We were both working on recovery and had just started trying to rebuild relationships with our combined five children that we had lost along the way. We both knew our families wouldn't welcome another baby.

In hindsight, I can see that God/Universe had a very exact plan for us. We both decided we were going to raise this new life and figure out a way to make it work. Both of us were very dedicated to never allowing this one to suffer like our others did. It was definitely not our plan, but we were both so blessed to be given this gift.

Around the same time, Bart had just escaped from an unpleasant situation. While I was away, a woman whose intentions I don't believe we're all bad, was sort of holding him hostage. He was in a terrible bike accident and needed a hip replacement. She took care of him so he could recover correctly. While he was healing, she had him classified as senile and took over responsibility for his financial and physical belongings and his decisions.

When he started feeling better, he snuck out and went to a lawyer. The lawyer could see he could care for himself and got everything out of her name and back into his. If I wasn't incarcerated, this wouldn't have happened. After all this man had done for me, I should've been there to take care of him.

My mother gave him my number after he contacted her. He quickly saw how good I was doing. He was thrilled with my growth. After all, he had always seen it inside of me. He wasn't thrilled about the pregnancy. However, he was happy that Jeremy was going to stand beside me.

Bart knew all too well that living in a trailer near Camden wasn't ideal. There has always been a correlation with losing my children and my addiction getting worse, so he wanted to make sure I stayed healthy. He knew I had a family living in Virginia that should be in this baby's life. He offered to help us purchase a house there.

Before I left the state, I had to get approval. I notified my officer where I was going and why. They granted me permission to look for houses for three days.

I found a local realtor and discussed the price range, and I sent her houses of interest. She had it all set up for us but wow it was a huge undertaking to look for, choose, and place a bid on a house in that short time frame.

After two exhausting days, we decided on one. It was a one hundred- and eighteen-year-old farmhouse. It was white with six bedrooms and it was seated on 2 acres of mountain land. The town of Big Island had a population of three hundred and fifty residents. I fell in love with its old charm and location.

We put a bid on it and returned home. Within a week we received a call that our bid was accepted. Wow, I felt like I was living in a dream almost too good to be true. Not even two years prior, I was a junkie praying for death. Now, it's as if by some miracle that I was given another chance at life.

A baby, a house, a faithful partner and it happened with unfathomable speed. It felt as if I was literally picked up from one life, brushed off and dropped into another. One that was more amazing than I could have ever dreamed. I finally found my own happily ever after.

CHAPTER 1.6 SOME FINAL TEST

I realize over the years that everything has to be in balance. There is a positive and negative to all things in life; order and chaos. My existence was no different.

Several things needed to happen before we could move. My patient probation officer could see my imperfect growth so when I told him about the house he agreed to let me finish October first. This would be a whole year early. A court date was set, and all I had to do was stay out of trouble until then.

Isaac, my oldest, turned eighteen on September twenty-fifth. He decided after careful thought that he would move down with us. I was grateful that he was giving me another chance. Things felt like they were falling right into place.

Jeremy had a daughter named Aiysha. She was two years older than my oldest. She too had been in and out of the system and at the time was living in an inpatient Psychiatric facility. Jeremy felt like it was time to step up and be more involved in her life. He checked her out without permission from his family.

Once again they weren't thrilled with us. We included her in the plan and the house was big enough for everyone. It saddened us that our other three kids wouldn't be eighteen for a long time but hopefully one day. Our wish would be for them to all be able to live together, but this would take a miracle.

With all my legal issues finally ending, I could relax a little. We only had two weeks to go. On top of that one of those weeks we planned on spending time at the beach with Jeremy's family. This would give me a chance to get to know the rest of them a little better.

Aiysha asked if she could see her mom, Hilda, before we moved three states away. It was a reasonable request, and we planned to accommodate. It had been many, many years since she had seen her so we thought it would be good for them to spend some time together prior to our departure. They made plans to go out the next day with Hilda's new boyfriend.

That morning, Jeremy and Ayisha, and I drove to pick up her mother and her mother's boyfriend. It had been a long time since I had seen Hilda myself as well. Jeremy and her dated back when I met him. Her and I were actually closer than Jeremy and I back then.

Jeremy dropped them off at a nearby shopping plaza so they could spend the day together shopping, eating and catching up. We drove them home and as we turned into their trailer park; we saw flashing lights behind us. Apparently, the rental car's license plate was wrong. It should've been a nice easy stop. They asked Jeremy for his identification and ran his name.

He had a felony probation violation for failure to report out of North Carolina from when he lived there with his sister. He told me about this before. We discussed having him turn himself in after the baby was born, however the universe had different plans.

They immediately put him in cuffs. His daughter was left in hysterics. She wasn't aware that her father had any outstanding warrants, but why would she? I was left feeling like what the fuck is going on. We were headed in the right direction and once again; I was all off course. When would I be able to catch a break?

We eventually got home and sat down to figure out how we would proceed. My mom had been visiting and agreed to stay to help with the move. Although she was scared, Aiysha decided she would still come too.

They took Jeremy to the nearest county jail until North Carolina came and got him. He connected with Eli from inside and asked if he would mind helping with the move and perhaps assist the family until he could get back to us. They had known each other as long as Jeremy and I so he agreed.

His family was even more upset at the whole situation than before but still wanted us to go on vacation with them. We had planned the Ocean City vacation for a year. Now that I was carrying their new grandchild I was included in the plan. They even invited my mom. With Jeremy incarcerated it was awkward for everyone. We had a nice time, but I would've been more comfortable with Jeremy there. The relationship I have with them could still use some work. Qué Será Será.

We rented a U-haul and Eli commissioned his two brothers to assist with loading the truck. I was now in my seventh month and I had caught a severe summer cold so I wasn't a great help.

Regretfully, Eli still was working on himself. Addiction isn't easy to live with and hard to manage. He tried to hide it from me, knowing it was imperative for me to stay clean. My heart broke for him–once you've lived that life you'll always know what that struggle looks like.

We started our caravan of cars. It was Eli and Isaac in the U Haul, my mom and I in our van. Then Bart and Aiysha in Isaac's car behind us. We all stopped and gassed up at the station. We got our drinks and snacks for the road and were all set to go.

My mom and I left first, expecting them all to be behind us shortly. Two hours later when we got to Maryland I got a phone call from Isaac. They were still at the gas station. Eli never came out and they couldn't find him in the store. I immediately knew what that meant; he either had nodded out in the bathroom or had overdosed.

I told Isaac he needed to go in and check. Gratefully, he found him asleep on the toilet. He came to and said he was constipated, but we all knew.

Issac informed me that Eli seemed lucid when he insisted it was time to go. I was already worried about Bart's advanced age, and my firstborn was in the car with his father in who knows what condition. To top it off, I was feeling sick at the moment and was having trouble breathing.

What should've been about a five-hour ride, took eight. We all were exhausted. I couldn't wait to get in, set up a bed and just sleep. Our beautiful one hundred- and eighteen-year-old house must have been perfectly staged because I didn't recognize it to be the same place I saw only a few months prior. I assumed it had been sitting abandoned from the day our offer was accepted.

My dream home was now a nightmare. It was deteriorating. The freshly painted walls were peeling. The mold and mildew that crawled in every corner was making it even harder to breathe. With no other option I asked the men to get my mattress and a window air conditioner out of the car so the kids and I had somewhere comfortable to sleep.

The next morning, we headed out to Walmart for cleaning supplies. On the way there, it was clear I needed a hospital, I could barely catch my breath. Eli dropped me off at the emergency room where I was admitted. I had pneumonia and my glucose levels were sky high. After further investigation, the doctors diagnosed me with preeclampsia and gestational diabetes.

Jeremy finally phoned and shared that they had transferred him to North Carolina and given bail, and I caught him up on the drama. I called around looking for bondsmen in the area. A company that was sympathetic to our situation, agreed to help us out. It didn't matter that we were being charged twenty percent instead of ten; I was just happy that anyone would bond him out. He lived out of state and the current violation was for leaving the state of North Carolina. Having him with me made life easier.

The next day, Eli and Bart went on a three-hour ride. Bart put up the bail, and Jeremy was released. We knew he would probably still have to go back, however a few months with him to help was better than nothing. Besides this would mean he could be present at the baby's birth.

Jeremy went and checked out the house and saw all the work that needed to be done. Then he came up to see me at the hospital. My mental state was almost as bad as my physical. They gave me steroids and had a terrible reaction. I was angry about the whole situation, but relieved to see him.

After a two-week stay in the hospital, I was released. They set me up with a local OB/GYN to be monitored weekly until the baby was born. We had to buy a blood pressure monitor, and they put me on insulin. However, I made it only to two of those appointments and at thirty-six weeks; I was back in the hospital. The goal was to get me to carry the baby to thirty-eight weeks, so it was safer to deliver.

Our little miss got stubborn and was breach and not flipping over. I was scheduled for a C-section, but one last ultrasound showed that she was ready to come to earth side. She had turned into position that same day.

We had a fairly easy birth and on November 20, 2018 we welcomed little Miss Bella Grace Dolce. She was our beautiful, sweet saving grace. I thought name suited her perfectly. I knew that moment forward there would be no going back to the ways of our old life.

Christmas that year came and passed. I got a part-time job at a local convenience store and started New Year's day. It was the only store in our town. I was happy to find something close. They sentenced the following week Jeremy to three months in a rehabilitation prison in North Carolina.

As you can imagine those three months were a struggle. I couldn't afford to get heating oil for the house. They wanted an eight hundred dollar minimum which was impossible to come up with. Our water came from a well we had never used before. So we heated the bedroom where I was staying with the baby. Then our water stopped working and with no prior knowledge of well water we did not know how to fix it. The family rotated working and watching Bella.

Our eighteen- and twenty-year-olds wound up with her most of the time. It was a tremendous learning experience for them. They did a great job. Eli started establishing new connections in town. He also took unannounced trips back and forth to NJ. It was clear the fresh start I hoped this would offer him did no such thing. He was getting worse physically, emotionally, and mentally. I knew I was going to end up losing my best friend.

Three months had passed, and it felt like that time would never end. Our family was back together. Isaac met a great guy named Danny and moved in with him about an hour away. I knew I would miss him but I didn't want to stop him at a chance at a life of his own.

That May, Jeremy asked me to go fishing.This was a common pastime we both enjoyed. He took me to the waterfall on the Blue Ridge Parkway. He asked me to get the small red hooks out of the tackle box. I did and noticed a ring box. I turned to look at Jeremy, and he was on one knee. He proposed, I said yes, and we both cried.

A few weeks later, I received a message from my sister's childhood best friend named Ursula. I knew her since she was about five. Her husband was in prison now. She and her five-year-old son, Turtle, needed somewhere to stay. I spoke with Jer and a few weeks later; we picked her up at the Greyhound station. She got a job and a car. Then in a few months her husband was released. We knew how blessed we were so we tried our hardest to bless as many others as we could.

We let him stay as well but only for a while. We needed a chance to have a house of our own. They were able to find a place in a couple of months. For the most part it seemed to have worked out well.

Hilda called and told us her boyfriend, Mike, had died from an overdose and she wasn't sure where she could live. We offered her a place without considering the consequences. I didn't want her to end up like Mike. She stayed in our house about a month before we knew she would have to rent a room somewhere else. She started acting bizarre. She walked around screaming at the people in her head. I wanted to be there for her through her grieving, but I couldn't let her live with us too long. I didn't want Bella to be exposed to the displays of mental illness that came with a lifestyle of drug abuse. My other kids had seen too much with me, and I learned from those mistakes.

Then 2019 happened. COVID hit and everything we knew was turned upside down. Around Halloween I had been waitressing at a new place. The money was better, but the owner was horribly mean. She would drag me table to table criticizing my every move in front of the customers. I was only planning on tolerating that until Christmas, but the following weekend I misread the schedule and I arrived an hour late. I was suspended and with that I decided to not return. Two days later, I received the news that the restaurant closed because several waitresses had fallen ill. I was spared, and I recognized this as a divine intervention immediately.

CHAPTER 1.7 MY SPONTANEOUS SPIRITUAL AWAKENING

Spiritual awakening is one of the hardest things to describe but understanding what it is has surely changed my life forever. I started having terrifying recurring dreams about being possessed. They all followed a similar theme. I'd be in a Large house with many rooms, searching for my Aunt Sharon's bedroom because it had a large tub. The house was always abandoned. I'd go upstairs and something invisible would fight to get into my body. It would lift me off the ground and I'd start screaming at it to try and exercise it out of me. I'd always get stuck to the ceiling. I'd call for Jesus and wake up in extreme fright.

This also happened on waking occasions as well. My face would begin to twitch and even contort. I'd exercise them also. I saw repeating numbers everywhere– 111,222,333 ect. It appeared I was receiving messages through music. I had an intense and insatiable desire to research everything and anything that would explain what was happening. Ultimately, I needed to know how the universe really works. I wanted to know that I existed and what was the purpose of it all.

I learned about meditation while attending The Therapeutic Learning Center. During meditation, I received messages, known to the spiritual common as downloads, to buy certain crystals and told to read specific books. They showed me pictures of people I never met; one time it was the current Dali Lama whom I'd never seen before. I went to search for information about the lost books of the Bible. I knew I was supposed to find the commonalities across different religions. I became obsessed.

Jeremy had to stop working for a little while to watch Bella because I started dissociating. I was physically present, but I was absent from most of what was going on around me. The only way I can explain it is how Charlie Brown from The Peanuts heard the adults around him–"Wah, wah, wah, wah."

Considering I was raised with a primarily catholic upbringing, not only was I petrified of this new awareness, but I knew nothing about spontaneous spiritual awakenings. For months I convinced myself that my many years of drug abuse had finally caused me to lose my mind. I kept hearing Mathew 7:7 "Seek and Ye shall find."

Looking back, I could recognize that I had been doing this my entire life. I had several otherworldly experiences before, but the fear of the unknown always led me back to drugs. Finally, my life was better than I ever saw possible so reverting to my old ways wasn't an option. I'd have to stand on my own two feet and walk blindly.

My sleep schedule changed. Between 3am and 4am, I would wake up. I had an unusual increase in energy. I looked up my symptoms. I related it to what was called a spiritual awakening but at the time there wasn't a lot of information on it. All the practitioners charged ridiculous amounts to even talk to you. We were both out of work so that wasn't an option.

At one point Jeremy asked me if I felt as though I needed a mental hospital. I already knew this routine. I explained what this entailed. Usually thirty-six hours of being strapped to a bed without a blanket in an empty room in only a gown for observation. I'd most likely be told I was having a manic episode and then I'd be heavily medicated.

Something deep in my soul was telling me it was time to see where my intense, insatiable curiosity was going to take me. I spent my entire life running from it and everyone could see how well that worked out for me. I'm so grateful Jeremy was so supportive–without him there to witness and verify what was happening to me I know people would've thought I was crazy. Without his dedication, my life would've continued to play on repeat.

Shadowy figures, flashing lights, and hearing people speak to me in my head happen more than occasionally. The voices were always in my voice but were not thoughts of my own. I feared that these symptoms were evil; I'd remember the messages I was hearing, and they were all positive. I kept a happy and excited feeling. Spirit kept telling me it was graduation time.

If I was losing my mind, at least it was affirmative crazy. When I have questioned my sanity in the past, it was because myself talking was telling me I was better off dead. This was unlike anything I experienced prior. How could being nicer to everyone and loving unconditionally be wicked?

One day as my face was contorting, it was twitching and my jaw was getting stuck open and crooked. I finally got it to stop. There was a shadow person at my door. I feared it was another demon and so I prepared for a mental attack. Five mins later, Ursula and her family knocked on the door. I realized it was a precognition of their unannounced visit.

Christmas this year differed from others. I'm usually super excited to play Santa. Holidays and wrapping gifts brought me closer to my childhood memories with Grammy, but I couldn't seem to get into it. Things didn't feel the same.

All the centuries of cover-ups made Christmas seem insignificant. I found out that most of our true history had been hidden. I discovered the way big brand food companies were packing their products with chemicals that make us sick. Fast-food restaurants were using compounds similar to plastics to fill the food we consume. I learned that television was used to program people and keep humans living in a state of fear.

I knew how important holiday celebrations were for the family so I pushed through the routine. I so badly wanted to feel my holiday joy. Life wouldn't be the same for me. Once I put on the glasses of awareness, I couldn't take them off. Once we see what is true in life instead of depending on society's explanations, there is no going back. Knowledge is definitely power, but the power to do what?

To my pleasant surprise, this Christmas turned into one of my most memorable ones. We had a great day–we spent time with the family opening gifts and eating. I received many nice gifts this year. Above all, my newly found spiritual gifts that really made it so special.

We had Hilda over for the holidays. Nobody deserves to be alone during the time of year families get together, and for all intents and purposes, Hilda was family. Hilda and I talked a lot, but the more I listened to the things she explained, I could see that she was spiritually awake although she had yet to realize it. She was so consumed by grief her symptoms were showing up differently.

On the way to her home, three huge reindeer crossed in front of our car. I don't think they're all that common in Virginia, especially downtown. This happened not once, but twice that day at two separate locations. I took this to be a sign, so I looked up the spiritual meaning of deers. They signify powerful sensitivity; they're a sign that you pick up on things that others don't.

Being that they crossed twice, that gave me the number thirty-three. Jeremy has always seen this number a lot. This is an important number. They taught me that this was the age of Jesus at his death. We have thirty-three vertebrae in our spine. There are also thirty-three degrees in the Freemasons. Its essence is also associated with new beginnings.

When we got home, we were exhausted by the hustle of the day. I sat on the couch and shut my eyes and saw a vision of someone in my head; it looked like a cartoon version of my dad in my third eye. Your third eye is believed to be in your pineal gland where your brain contains crystals that vibrate. It's what allows us to have visions.

I could communicate with my father and could feel his energy, the same as when he walked in a room when he was alive. He spoke to me telepathically and told me I had to forgive him.

This message confused me. We had been building a close relationship when he passed. I assumed I had fully forgiven him. I really tried to feel into the message. As an adult, I was so happy he was doing well and wanted me in his life; however, there was a part of me that was still hurt and felt unworthy of love.

Healing occurs in layers. Although I had put a few years into recovery, I understood I was still in need of healing. I had to take an unbiased look at everything that led into my addiction. There were times I had to confront a situation and assume it was resolved. It crept back up and had to be healed on a deeper level.

I had to stop judging everyone. When reviewing my trauma it was as if I could see things from the point of views of others. I could understand that everyone was doing the best that they knew how. This helped me become less judgemental and able to love more fully without conditions.

Sometimes, I felt like I was being a sissy.I knew many others have had it much worse than myself. I knew I would have to learn to love myself. I finally knew it wasn't selfish to love yourself. I had always been my own harshest critic. I practiced daily, sometimes hourly affirmations. *I'm safe, I'm loved. I'm protected, I'm worthy.*

For me, forming boundaries with others is being able to identify when someone or something isn't healthy for me. There will be people that look at you and can only see the older version of you and the pain that you caused. I knew at least for the time being there were going to be some people that I had to cut out of my life.

It was very painful and very necessary. I would have to first fully heal before I could help with those I had hurt along the way. Being spiritually aware doesn't erase the burden of your past, and you can keenly see what you were blind to before. Learning to set boundaries was something I had to learn to do in order to remain good to myself at the same time I was mending the relationships that were damaged with my drug abuse. I started with my longtime friends, Eli and Hilda.

Eli had an attraction to Hilda and hadn't really dated in many years. So when he asked us if Hilda could move back in we hesitantly agreed. Their effort at a relationship lasted barely a week.

Tensions grew in the house, and Hilda moved out of his room. With nowhere else to go we let her move upstairs to Aiysha's old bedroom.

Being that she and I were going through similar experiences and having visions as well, I decided I'd read her cards.

I set up on the floor with a candle and my crystals. Hilda and I sat across from each other cross-legged, and I suggested she meditate with me prior so I could connect to her energy. I put a healing frequency on my speaker. We shut our eyes. I instructed her to breathe in her nose and out her mouth. I advised her to focus on her breathing to clear her mind.

I was deep in meditation when I saw an immense, long black figure that crawled on its six legs. This thing had bright red glowing eyes. Frankly, it creeped me out, and I decided I would not read her cards. If whatever that thing was, is connected to her energy, I wanted no parts of it.

This disturbing vision was a definite sign that I needed to put down a solid boundary in my relationship with her.

In the spring of 2021 there were no signs of the Covid restrictions ending. We had been putting off the wedding, hoping to have both of our entire family's attend. Instead, we decided to get a cabin in the woods of Tennessee and have someone marry us in the presence of our immediate family.

The wedding was beautiful and stress free. Ursula was my maid of honor and Kenny was Jeremy's best man. I got my hair professionally done in long curls. I wore a stunning strapless off white lace gown. We made wild flower crowns for Bella and I. I got to see Jeremy in a suit for the first time. It was a black suit with a yellow vest and tie. We had written our own vows. Afterwards we danced and had fireworks. My mom's best friend, Kathy, treated us all for dinner. It was perfect.

Eli and Hilda were still a large part of our life but we didn't want to bring the energy of prior failed relationships into our marriage. We asked them to find an alternate living situation. That didn't go over well. Eli immediately packed up his belongings and started sleeping in his car across the street. I suppose it was to make us feel guilty, but I needed to stand firm in this decision no matter how Eli felt.

When the guilt trip didn't work, he trashed our reputation to the neighbors. He called Isaac and told him I kicked him out with nowhere to go. This wasn't at all the case. We didn't intend to end our friendship with Eli and Hilda, so we gave them a couple months to look for a place. Eli didn't understand the reasoning behind our decision since they had been a part of our lives for so long, but addicts find it hard to place other's desires over their own.

Jeremy and I were newly married, and Eli took out Hilda and got her high. She had been trying hard to make better choices for herself. Although he didn't hold a gun to her head, the offer was too tempting for her to refuse. They broke my one rule in the house–No hard drugs.

When Eli asked us to let her move back in, we told him drug use of any kind would be the deal breaker. We had him live with us for three years and we knew nothing we could do to get him to stop. He didn't need to bring her back down as well.

Isaac and I had remained extremely close, even at my lowest. He ran away from every foster home the state placed him. Somehow Eli's sadness triggered him, making all the pain I caused him in his childhood to resurface.

Isaac contacted me and berated me as a mother, reminding me of every terrible thing I'd ever done. He said I was a horrible person and insisted that although I was clean, my controlling behavior still hadn't changed. He told me I was no better, even without the drugs.

My emotions went haywire. I was trying to set boundaries so that I could be a better mother and now I was blindsided with all the sadness and guilt from my past. I knew that there wasn't anything I could do to change my past. All I could do was be the best version of me here and now. If he felt that I was still a bad person, I didn't know what to do about it.

I remember the raging pain I held towards my mother for many years so I understood Isaac's feelings, even though it hurt. He told me if I really loved him I'd stay out of his life.

I knew how blessed I was to have another chance with Bella, but Isaac's tirade made me question my ability to be a good mother to her. I feared that I'd ruin her life as well. Since He had insisted I was just as bad without the drugs then perhaps it was a fault in my personality and not just my addiction that caused him all the pain. If Isaac needed time, I'd give it to him. I decided I wouldn't push. I couldn't let myself get swallowed by an old definition of who I was, even if the separation was going to kill me. I hope one day he can forgive me.

The more I healed the more in-tune I became with my spiritual gifts. My dad wasn't the only one talking to me from the other side.

Nenenanny, my great grandma, visited me as well. I could feel her around me. We'd been talking to Eli's dad on the telephone. Nanny always had a little crush on him. I giggled as I felt the excited energy she used to get when she was around him. She told me that if she knew then what she knew now, she would've lived differently. When she felt my sadness she told me not to be sad and that we'd be having toast and tea again soon. I did not know how we'd be able to do that but found great comfort in knowing it to be true.

Staying grounded has always been a problem for me. The more often I let myself spend time in my head the harder this was for me. Time in nature became imperative for me. The family took many trips to the woods or went to sit by the creeks. Spirit definitely placed us in the perfect location for this. We even decided we would start growing some of our own food.

I got a job at the Ruby Tuesday's in Bedford just down the mountain from the house. It wasn't really a money thing; I needed to keep my mind occupied. As our conscious mind begins to expand, you begin to question reality. You need to be in the world, but not of it.

Mental health has always been a concern in my life. I'd never heard voices prior to all this. All the thoughts are in my voice. Schizophrenia sets in late teens and early twenties. I'm well aged and passed this possibility.

The solitary half-hour drive from our house to work gave me the chance to differentiate the diverse voices in my head. I noticed my ego was the defensive, old-way-of-thinking voice that I usually heard on my left. Whereas my higher self was on my right and would give me guidance.

I tuned in more to the guidance I received and acted on it. I was informed who I should share my experiences with. On many occasions my ego would argue back about how crazy I was going to appear to others. Each time I acted on this, I'd receive confirmation from the other person. They'd be surprised with the timing and accuracy of the unsolicited advice.

I followed the patterns in my ups and downs. I'd be stable and in tune with the natural and spiritual world and then like the drop of a hat I would feel like my life was out of control. I'd have a lot of unwarranted drama surrounding me. At times, actually most of the time, it came from the people closest to me. I'd have a far drop back in the progress I had made.

During those times, I was directed toward areas of my life I still needed to address. I could work through the lessons I kept missing in my life. Once I figured out what I needed to learn, I'd make peace with things. I was then flung forward into more discoveries and self realizations. But remaining in a state of faith over fear had to become my new normal.

I learned that most of my dreams had some sort of meaning. So, when I had a dream that Jeremy had sex with a woman from town, I was irate. I immediately questioned him, even knowing it was only a dream, and he seemed very nervous about my dream.

His actions had been erratic. He was always working either at the house or at someone else's. With his Obsessive Compulsive Disorder (OCD) this wasn't uncommon. However, he wasn't sleeping much and seemed to nod out. I feared a relapse but when I questioned him, he angrily denied it.

A few days later, Aiysha was over and she was acting standoffish. I asked her if she thought her dad was using again and she broke down crying. She was scared to tell me he had been doing Suboxone for a few months.

The same woman in my dream was the one he had been purchasing the drugs from. Boy, do I wish I was more effective at interpreting my dreams. Perhaps I could've stopped it sooner. Aiysha asked me not to tell him but I had no choice— my new life was at stake.

I confronted Jeremy, and he didn't deny it. I was grateful for his honesty, yet I still felt very betrayed. When we first started dating, I had two firm rules— Any drug use would be the reason for the immediate end to our relationship. The second, of course, was cheating; that was unforgivable.

I left our home and went to my mom's for a few nights. I was heartbroken. Not so much that he slipped up, but more so that he didn't trust me enough to come to me about it. It took a good few months for us to recover from this deception and a couple years for me to fully trust him again.

This was a terrible experience for both of us and actually brought us closer. He learned that I'm there for him no matter what, and I learned a lesson in forgiveness. Yet another lesson became a blessing.

I hadn't taken very good care of my teeth throughout my addiction. I'd brush if I had access to running water but it had been about twenty years since I had seen a dentist. So it was no surprise when I had to go to a dentist for a severe toothache in the back of my mouth.

State dental insurance is next to non-existent in Virginia. We eventually found an office that would pull it out. I wish that was the worst of it however upon reviewing my X-rays they discovered a small tumor. It was at the top of my gum inside my sinus cavity. The dentist showed concern, which really frightened me.

He wasn't able to do anything about it there, so he gave me a referral. The only place that would cover the procedure had a two-year waiting list. I went on a year-long search for someone to help me. I went to the Ears, Nose, Throat doctors who kept referring me to the orthodontic surgeons. I saw six different physicians and paid out of pocket only to get the same responses. They didn't want to remove it in fear that I'd permanently lose the feeling in the front of my face. I can't say I blame them; they didn't want to be responsible for those kinds of damages.

We gave up on looking for help from doctors. I'd been learning about reiki energy and I asked the angels to help remove the tumor. I knew I had energy I could feel flowing through my hands. In China and other cultures this energy is called Chi. I took the Chi energy and slowly made a circular motion in the tumor's spot. Jeremy and I had faith and believed I was healed, allowing us to stop worrying about it.

One day, I was sitting on the couch and playing on my phone. For whatever reason, Hilda was video taping me on her phone. She showed me the video. It showed me on the couch looking down at the phone; however, to both our utter shock in my voice you could hear me say "Hi Hilda". I never spoke or looked up from my phone. How was this possible? It was, as if, my higher self had spoken.

Hilda and I had a very intense connection. She was the mother of Jeremy's oldest two children and our friendship was rocky. We bonded over the fact that we were both experiencing an awakening that no one else around us truly understood.

I later had a dream that I was at a hospital. People were going crazy. There was a lot of screaming and crying. It appeared as if their physical appearances were changing. I went to the hospital staff and tried to explain that we were experiencing the "Great Awakening." The staff had the doctors evaluate me and I was taken and locked in a room for observation. While I was being held, I saw Hilda. She turned into a reptilian alien with two tongues and began trying to fight me.

When I woke up, I told Jeremy about this dream. I knew that the first part was addressing my concerns about how other people were reacting to my newfound understanding and my fears of their opinion.

Just then Hilda walked into my bedroom. She already wasn't happy with us because she had to find her own place, she then told me she and Jeremy were talking about his past intimacy with someone else. She went on, angrily giving me excuses why she had said nothing to me before, claiming she wanted to stay out of our relationship. It was a mistake to think that our connection was stronger. I believed she should've alerted me if she had a concern of him not being satisfied by me.

I don't think she was an angry, green monster. The message expressed she was talking back and forth between Jeremy and I behind my back. Hence her having two tongues. I rarely receive point blank messages, they all seem to be encoded. I understood what the symbols meant. Spirit seemed to speak to me in this manner.

We thought Hilda would get a motel since she had not applied for any rentals. We wanted to help her, but not from inside our own home. She lingered as if she didn't believe that we were serious. Instead of looking for a place in town while she had a chance, she thought going back to New Jersey was a better option. I was concerned about her choice but it wasn't my life to live. What happened to her afterward is her story to share.

"First, you be the dream, then you live the dream." I knew that I had a life purpose. I had always had a deep knowing I was here for a reason. I remember when I was at my worst, telling Isaac that perhaps my purpose was to have him and Trinity so they could fulfill their purpose. At that point, I had given up on my own dreams. I knew I was here to help others overcome the same obstacles that I had. I didn't know how, yet I knew I had to be fully healed before I could attempt to take this one.

Spirit directed me to once again to reevaluate my childhood. I got frustrated by this request. How many times was I going to have to do this? I was reminded if I was to wander into the woods and walk for ten years; how long did I suppose it would take me to walk back? Meaning if I walked a thousand miles it would take a thousand miles to walk back home. I couldn't expect a few years in recovery to reconstruct a lifetime of damage. I realized I had to fully heal to help others heal.

One thing I did to begin my healing process was to write a letter to my mom. She's still alive and Mommy and I have a better relationship with her. I didn't want to rehash old feelings. Later, I burnt that letter to give a visual of releasing the feelings that held me to the past once and for all.

I thought I worked through everything with Ricky, but I knew there was the little one in me who hadn't. So, I wrote to him as if I was still that little girl who needed her daddy so badly.

A few days later, I saw it was going to be May 6th, the day I had baby Elise, my still born Angel. I called work and told them I wouldn't be in and explained why. I had the best boss, and she understood. I attempted to do this while I was in treatment.

The counselors had planned a treat for us–they were going to take us to the beach. We were asked to write a letter about a situation we were ready to let go of. They stopped at the store and purchased balloons for us. We sat in a circle and read our letters out loud. I wrote mine to Elise. Afterwards we all let go of the balloons. It should've been beautiful. Welp, that worked for the rest but my balloon headed over to a nearby hotel balcony and got stuck. The occupants came out and brought the balloon and my letter.

I laughed over the irony, but quickly turned into sobs. It was proof to me I wasn't ready to release it yet. So this time I just sat on my porch and wrote to her. I apologized to her and cried out loud. As I made peace with Elise, I heard bells ring out of nowhere as I finished writing. It was a magical experience. It made me think of the quote from the movie, It's a Wonderful Life– "Every time a bell rings, an angel gets its wings"

Ten years ago, when I was still in addiction, I began writing my story. I had gotten ten chapters in before I knew my story wasn't over. I abandoned the idea like I had everything else in my life. This time, I knew what I had to do–I had to fully trust in God to show that I was dedicated.

So, my first step in demonstrating my faith was to call my job and tell them I wouldn't be back. I gave them the honest reason why. I knew I didn't have to worry about money and that God would find a way. He/She always had.

During this journey, I had to let go of many people in my life and I was getting lonely. I started a few new endeavors, but nothing had fallen into place. Then suddenly I found a spiritual group called Connecting Consciousness. I heard about them through TikTok. It was based out of the United Kingdom, luckily it had a branch in Virginia.

They invited me to a local meeting in the next town over. Then, another group, the Convention of States, was having a meeting right in our small town's library. From making friends at that meeting I learned that they actually had a writing group as well. Once the old energy is cleared out, it brings in the people that match the frequency of your new energy.

Another development in this journey was communication with Trinity. I had only seen her once in the last seven years and one day I received a text from her. She was angry, hurt and depressed, and I completely expected she would be. I was just happy that she reached out. She wanted to meet her sister and wanted me to be more present in her life. I never felt deserving of her love. I know I can't fix my past mistakes but now I can be there for her. Wow, it is so beautiful. Once you start healing, the things you lost actually come back. I hope she will heal as well. I never thought I would see this day.

Jeremy's son, Peyton, had been living with his aunt for the last three years and had just turned ten. His mom hadn't been in his life for a long time. He lived with his aunt. One day, she called, saying she heard Jeremy was back on his feet. She invited us to come to Pennsylvania to visit with Peyton as he was struggling from being without his parents. Arrangements were made for Peyton to come and spend time with the family for Easter, and then again for the summer. Before the summer was over, his aunt gave us custody. Things were definitely falling into place for us.

One day, I sat down to eat dinner and bit into a piece of corn on the cob. My front tooth finally gave out and broke. It didn't come out clean, so I had to make a dentist appointment. The technicians took x-rays of my mouth. The doctor informed me that two teeth needed to be pulled. I asked the dentist to review the images to see if the tumor they saw at an earlier appointment was still there. She looked at me as if I were crazy. Miraculously, the tumor was no longer there. I was so excited and grateful, and still in utter shock. I was so astounded that I asked for a copy to compare with the old ones.

I'm still amazed by this miracle. However, missing these teeth was an enormous embarrassment for me. I had to choose between following Spirit's guidance and publishing my book or paying for a partial plate to replace my missing teeth. Once again, I was yanked back to learning to love myself no matter what I look like. Universe may have just possibly spared my life once again. So, until I finish my spirit lead task, I'll be learning a lesson in confidence.

To make things even more unbelievable, I reached out to Isaac. We hadn't spoken in nearly two years. He was willing to accept me back into his life. All I lost to the darkness was being returned.

CHAPTER 2.1 MY INNERSTANDINGS

Let's Explore Spirituality Together

I've shared my journey through this physical existence this far. Now, I'm going to give my personal explanation of how and why this is happening and the possibilities of what I see on the horizon for my place and purpose in this life. Perhaps, when you look around, you have questions about what's happening in this time and space that we know to be the world. My guess is you have an inkling that the world has been off.

This is what I've learned through my years of research of sacred text, learning of new discoveries, meditation, and inner knowing. Please understand that my experience will differ from yours, so what I'm sharing with you is my personal truth. Truths can be very subjective; there isn't one truth that is fully right or wrong. There are many ways to get to the same destination.

We all grew up on fairy tales with dragons, angels, elves, witches, fairies and such. Our minds have been taken off too far-away lands, and we've believed in magic and thought anything was possible. Once we start school, around the young, impressionable age of four or five, they teach us to sit down, be quiet, and pay attention to what we are taught in our history. Our imagination takes a back seat while we learn to obey what we see and hear.

Language and meaning is important to human development. Let's consider two words here. First History, "his" and "story", which is exactly what it sounds like. The victor writes history, usually a man. We're taught one side of the truth through a filtered lens or a complete lie in order for us to continue down the propagated trajectory.

Now, let's look at the word Imagination. "I"- "Magi "- "Nation". Who are the Magi? They were Zoroastrian priests with supernatural powers. They were astrologists, alchemists and magicians. They are found in the Bible bringing infant Jesus gifts as described in Matthew 2 known as the visit of the three wise men.

Perhaps we should live in our imagination and bringing it forth into our physical existence. That's what I'm doing now by writing this book. Ask yourself what makes reality real? It could be nothing more than our perception that's informed by our lived experience. Each situation filters through life, affecting our thoughts. We're not our past experiences. We're not our thoughts. We are not our emotions. If we aren't any of these things, what are we? I'm so glad you asked - we are the observers.

This concept can be hard to comprehend, but if we don't understand this, our lives will continue to repeat the same stories until we do. Hearing the same story repeatedly makes us believe that it's true. If we react the same way every time the situation arises, but expect a different outcome that's what we call insanity.

CHAPTER 2.2 MENTAL ILLNESS

In this chapter, I'd like to discuss mental illness for a moment. The majority of my life I've been diagnosed with one type of disease or another. I'd like to suggest a more holistic way to treat anyone who could not fit in a box, those who are often misunderstood due to their ultra sensitive nature.

If you could imagine that your body is an antenna. We're constantly sending out signals through our emotions. E-motions are energy in motion. We attract the same frequency that we emit.

Most people's antennas are shut down between the ages of five to seven. When I was researching on the National Library of Medicine website, I noticed that this is when our brain waves go from theta, which is a meditative programmable state, to alpha which is the analytical mind.

In cases that your antenna doesn't shut off, one may display behavior that isn't to be "expected". When your antenna remains on you are more perceptive. Your imagination is more vivid. Sometimes you may have a hard time relating to others. Believe it or not, your imagination can provide you with clear vision and therefore clear thinking.

When we feel that something is wrong with our health, we go to the doctor. This usually begins the road down experimental, petroleum-based medications. One medicine or a combination of prescriptions that may or may not relieve the symptoms that are causing the undesirable behavior.

Have you ever listened to a commercial for antipsychotic drug treatments? I have. The list of side effects is mind-boggling. This solution may be suitable for a temporary fix, however the side effects can be worse than the original problem–suicidal ideations, numbness, and constant nausea are amongst the most common.

Most prescriptions stop feelings of anxiety, but they also halt feelings of hope, joy, love, excitement. This isn't healthy. It can cause indifference and a lack of empathy.

Through The Universal Laws of Vibration and Attraction we're only going to keep perpetuating the loop. We'll talk about The Universal Laws later in the book. Without proper education we will remain in a lower vibration. Instead, we should learn about the twelve universal laws and how to use them to our advantage to get out of these vicious cycles.

"You're crazy."

"What's wrong with you?"

"Why can't you be normal?" These types of questions create a belief that something is wrong when in actuality, our "normal" is different and untethered by the boundaries of the scripted reality. If doctors keep their patients heavily medicated, they keep them in the theta, programmable state of mind. The frequencies you send out are the same that will come back to you. Low frequencies equal depressing kinds of experiences. Higher frequencies bring about more joyful experiences.

A person diagnosed with schizophrenia faces uncomfortable and often traumatic symptoms of the disease–they hear and talk to aliens, military personnel, demons, or whatever may be the case. Maybe, just maybe, they're spiritually gifted, but are unaware and untrained on how to wield that power. Who would want to be plagued like that? The easiest way to "help" them is to medicate them, but then they are often made fun of, and passed over by society.

Because of antipsychotic medications, the lower frequencies never shuts off. They tune into lower dimensions of reality, which basically means that all that CAN be seen is darkness and sadness. It's imperative to learn to change the radio station, so to speak, to raise the vibration to tune into the inner guidance, and therefore see brighter realities.

In many native cultures, people who show symptoms of this type of disease are taken under the wings of shamans and taught to connect with Ancestors and God. They're able to live productive lives and assist many others with their gifts.

CHAPTER 2.3 WHY IS ALL THIS HAPPENING

Many will say humanity is in the "end times". They could be right, as there are as many end time prophecies as there are origin stories. It makes no difference if we're looking at the Hopi seventh fire, the book of revelations, or the Mayan calendar's end. The tale is all the same. Humanity will come to a time when evil is so prevalent in our world we will have to make a choice to either continue down the same path we're on and Mother Nature will have to clean up the mess we've made or we can come together and create Heaven on Earth.

The "New Age Movement" calls this the fifth dimension. You may have heard it referred to as "The Golden Age" or "The Age of Aquarius". It's all referring to the same thing. This is the time we're experiencing now. How blessed are we to be living amid human evolution?

The word Apocalypse, according to the dictionary, actually means revelation. A revelation is the act of revealing or disclosing. Yes, during this era, everything must fall apart in order to be re-built and built better. Fear of the unknown and uncomfortable has kept many from accepting the inevitable–we must rebuild. Jesus communicated to people as parables. Parables are simple stories that have moral lessons. His teachings were considered heresy, so he used symbolism to share the information so that only the people who were on his frequency could understand, and evade the consequence of death.

We should view the Book of Revelations in this same context. It's possible that the seven lamps are, in actuality, the seven chakras within our body.

To take it a step further, let's consider the seals to be levels of consciousness. Scripture in the Bible describes them as being opened in this order:

First seal, a crown is given, which would be reconnection to Source/God. This is directly linked to our subconscious.

Second seal, a sword is given with the ability to discern good from evil. You no longer need safety in numbers. It's independence. According to the Gia channel, A spiritual based application< thirty percent of humanity resides here.

Third seal is balance, questioning myths. This could be logical conscious awareness. When this seal opens, we're no longer tied to the pain and suffering of our lived experience. We understand duality.

Fourth seal, power was given, this could be thought of as the ability to see many perspectives or visions. It's a bridge between the upper and lower levels of consciousness. Once open, it represents unconditional love and absolute amnesty.

Fifth seal showed us souls that were slain for the word of God; fears conquered by love. Think of it as Superconsciousness and the end of dualistic thinking.

At the opening of the Sixth seal, the earthquakes and the stars fall. The veil is thinned and you can travel in and out of our bodies. Our kundalini energy is activated. The kundalini is a Hindu term. It's the divine female energy that is at the bottom of our spine. Once activated, it travels the spine through all of our chakras. This is also called Christ consciousness.

The Seventh seal of silence is followed by wars and plagues. This could be viewed as confronting all of these imperfections or our dark self. A spiritual union with the Creator. We realize that we and Source are one and the same. It's the state of enlightenment!!!

Christ consciousness is self-actualization. It's the realization of the higher self in a universal system. It's a union with God and the Divine. Living and acting in a state of unconditional love to everyone and everything. I'm coming to believe that Christ has returned, and he's in the hearts and minds of those who choose to do the work and put aside all judgment.

My point of view is only one of many perspectives. Please, use your own discernment as I don't want to lead anyone astray. I only hope to broaden your perspective so that you can read the message of the End Day prophecies and interpret on your own. I believe many have pure intentions. However, we can't blindly follow the leader when looking for the truth.

The Bible has been revised so many times and it's unfortunate, especially when it clearly states throughout scripture itself that changing the word of God is unacceptable. It can be found in Revelations 22:18-19

"I warn everyone who hears the words of the prophecy of this book: if anyone adds to them, God will add to him the plagues described in this book, and if anyone takes away from the words of the book of this prophecy, God will take away his share in the tree of life and in the holy city, which are described in this book." Two hundred years ago, nineteen books were removed by the Council of Nicea. If that isn't changing God's word, I don't know what is.

Proverbs 30: 5-6 *"Every word of God is flawless;*
He is a shield to those who take refuge in him.
Do not add to his words,

or he will rebuke you and prove you a liar."

Just to reference a few. Not all the changes were done maliciously. The Bible was translated from its original Aramaic language to Hebrew then to Greek into Latin, and eventually into English. A lot can be lost through that many interpretations. It wouldn't surprise me if some meanings were changed on purpose in order to maintain control of the people who couldn't own a Bible–they had to believe whoever gave the message. After all kings, queens, rulers, and politicians all need laborers. If all the "commoners" had equal access to esoteric knowledge, who would clean their toilets?

Over the centuries, secret societies have broken off and gone into hiding with many truths. The Knights of Columbus, The Templars, Freemasons, and the Order of the Blue Rose just to name a few. However exclusive these groups are, at least the knowledge has been preserved.

Prior to my spiritual awakening, I had no knowledge such a thing existed. How could it be one day you're going about business as normal and the next you're crying over how your whole life has been a lie battling seemingly invisible forces? Why in the western world are we not prepared for this? Where are the therapists trained in spontaneous awakenings?

Once this starts, there's no going back. You're open to a whole new existence beyond this one. Many times it left me yearning to go back to the mundane. It's true when they say that ignorance is bliss, but then so is knowing.

I was thrown spiraling down endless rabbit holes in search of answers. Even now that I have a general idea of the how's, who's, and why's of some of this, it always seems I'm one answer away from understanding. Then I go in search of the answer I thought I was looking for and end up with another question. It's a never-ending cycle.

When COVID-19 first hit the nation, we were all sent into lockdown. This allowed people time to ponder. I've noticed a huge increase in awakenings in humanity over the last few years. Even those who have yet to experience this to the extreme, can mostly agree our world is desperately in need of change. The governments have caused great division amongst us. We're killing ourselves, each other, and the Earth.

At some point Mother Nature will say enough is enough. This has happened before and always ends in disaster. There is thought to be a comet that killed off the dinosaurs. There was a flood in the times of Noah. A mud flood that ended the Tartarian era. We can't forget the Ice Age. All which were brought on by the polar shift like the one we're beginning to experience now. Melting ice caps, floods, and droughts worldwide are signs of this shift.

It's my belief that our Creator doesn't want this to happen again. Perhaps this is why so many of us are awakening to truths. We're discovering our mission to help. We're spread far and wide and strategically placed so we can spread the word to help awaken others and support them on their journey. Then they too can discover their own purpose.

I'm not trying to push my beliefs onto others. I only attempt to share with you the information I've discovered during my journey hoping It sparks something for you to research for yourself. Signs, wonders, and messages all must be interpreted with your heart, not your mind. Our minds have been programmed. Our ego interprets past experiences as a guide and tries to protect us. If our ego hasn't been healed, its protection mechanism can be misleading and could lead us to fear an outcome that is more beautiful than the pain.

I really enjoy pulling apart words. Here are a few to think about. What do we watch on tv? Programs, right? TV is television. Tell-lie-vision. The tell lie vision is what they used to program us. The powers that be attempt to keep us in a state of fear and distraction.

They've put all the truths about what they're doing right in our faces; until now, we've never really looked or reasoned why.

For instance, the Jesuits took over the Vatican In 1534. Vatican as in Vedic. Vedic which is Hindu sacred text. The same information or core values from the Hindu text formed into the parables is in our Holy Bible. The initiates of secret societies and mystery schools understood this. It left the rest of us seeking outside of ourselves for God. Who are the Jesuits anyway? It's the Roman Catholic Church.

I don't wish to place my judgment and rant over one religion or the next as it isn't my job to judge others. However, most are familiar with the nauseating amount of cover-ups within that religious organization regarding children. Not as many are aware of the tens of thousands of native children's bodies buried on the lands of the boarding schools owned by the church in the Americas and Canada. I can now see why I had an aversion to my eighth-grade confirmation. I'm pleased with the decision I made.

I've always believed in Jesus and his teachings. Something deep down also led me to believe in reincarnation. Until I started studying the lost text, I couldn't quite put the two together. I understood that scientifically energy couldn't be created or destroyed, but I never knew the logistics of how that worked. My understanding now breaks it down like this: There's one God. He/she is conscious and has always existed this way. This consciousness is in all of life. It's everywhere and everything. God is all-knowing without form nor physical sense.

This consciousness separated pieces of itself into masculine and feminine in order to create. It created sound frequency and light. These rays of light are separated in angles also known as angels. Then created into patterns called Sacred Geometry forming into the Universe. The Universe holds many distinct patterns and frequencies. Each galaxy is filled with planets. Each planet is filled with many species. This continues through all time and space.

CHAPTER 2.4 METAPHYSICS IN THE BIBLE

This could make you feel insignificant in the grand scheme, but it's the exact opposite. This means we too are fractals of this light; Children of God. Jesus even reminded us of this when persecuted in John 10:34 "Is it not written in your law that you are all gods" he was referring to Psalms 82:6. "Ye are gods"

We can look at Romans 8:17 "We are God's children and if his children also heirs-heirs of God and co-heirs with Christ - if indeed we suffer with him we will be glorified with him" The word "Christ" dates way prior to Jesus' life.

The word Christ or Kryst means the anointed one. It comes from the Greek word Christos. In Sanskrit it's Krista which means, "cosmic attractor" or Krishna which is a name for God Almighty.

Let's take another look at the antenna analogy. One could hypothesize that Jesus was sent to us with his antenna on and was correctly trained with gnosis, or spiritual knowledge, from the age twelve until around thirty. In Catholic school, I learned it's called an agnostic church. A few years ago, I researched this and discovered Gnostic means "knowing", whereas agnostic means "not knowing." Why in the world would one choose to be ignorant? They've put all this information right in our faces the whole time, and then fear that we'll learn what it is we're really doing. Jesus was trying to teach us the knowledge that he had studied during the missing years that aren't found in the books. Perhaps he was even killed and demoralized for it.

What was this knowledge that he and his apostles tried to teach us? 1 Corinthians 11:11 "Be imitator of me, as I am Christ."

Ephesians 4:22-24–"That in reference to your former manner of life, you lay aside your old self, which had been corrupted with lust and deceit, and that you be renewed in the spirit of your mind, and put on they new self, which in the likeness of God has been created in righteousness and holiness of truth." To be Godly is to be love. John 4:8 states, "God is love."

How can we be love and lay aside our former life? I needed to start with forgiving and healing. This means everyone and everything that we have ever experienced are to be forgiven. I had to take an inventory of my whole life. I had to take responsibility for my part of it. I acknowledged that everyone did the best that they could with the knowledge and understanding that they held at the time. I believe most people try to do the best they can.

The most difficult part of this was forgiving myself for the pain that I caused to others. I recognized we repeat patterns we're taught until we see them. Once we detect the cycles, we can break them. This breaks generational traumas and can heal our ancestral line.

I identify as Spiritual. All religions have similarities. I hope to open others' eyes to this. In this day and time we need to unite. Another way they try to separate us is through race war, political views, gender, and sexual preferences. The way and details of how we live as love is not of importance. Just as long as we can all get there together.

We don't own television, and we have well watered. I didn't see that as a gift but I do now. Not having service slowed down the information that was programming us to societal norms and kept us in fear. The well water is not full of chemicals or added fluoride.

Fluoride calcifies the pineal gland. They have also added it to food and toothpaste to keep it dormant.

Why is the pineal gland so important? Read Genesis 32:30 "And Jacob called the place Pineal. For I have seen God face to face, and I have been delivered." There's a frequency we can listen to, 963 hz, which helps vibrate the crystals found in this gland to help restore it. The pineal gland, also known as the third eye, is part of the chakra system. It's considered being the sixth chakra.

Before doing this, I suggest you work on the other Chakras first. You should start at the bottom and work your way up. This can be done in a variety of ways, most which include meditation.

CHAPTER 2.5 THE CHARKRA SYSTEM

Let's talk about Chakras, which are energy centers in our body. They are supposed to spin in clockwise circular motions. Each is associated with a color and corresponds with nerves and major organs. There are many, but seven primary ones. These start at the base of your spine and go to the top of your head.

The **Root Chakra** is also known as the **Muladhara**. It's the color Red. The Root Chakra is associated with organs of elimination. It's at the pelvis and extends down to the bottom of your feet. This includes the large intestine, bladder, kidneys, rectum, bottom of the feet and sciatic nerves.

This chakra, when working properly, allows us to feel secure and grounded. Our early childhood can affect or imbalance this chakra. An imbalance can cause anxiety. We can work to correct this through yoga, food, smell, crystals, affirmations, frequency and meditation. Inner child meditations work well for this one.

If you like aromatherapy try sandalwood, rosewood, cedarwood, cypress, ginger, cinnamon and cloves. Think about earthy tones. Putting your feet directly in the ground can help. As for foods, the general rule of thumb is eat the same color as the chakra. Nature is the best teacher. So you could introduce tomatoes, strawberries, raspberries, cherries, red apples and peppers, pomegranate and beets into your diet.

The crystals that could help are hematite, black obsidian, and garnet. Try repeating that I'm safe. I'm grounded. I'm healthy. Listen to the frequency of 396 Hz. Over time you'll physically be able to feel if your chakras are open and spinning correctly. If they aren't, you'll have to go back and work on it. Until you can feel them on your own, you can hold a pendulum over the chakra and see how it is spinning.

The second chakra is the **Sacral chakra**. It's also known as the **Svadhishthana.** It's the color Orange. It's associated with creativity, sexuality and emotions. If it's blocked, it causes fear, especially fear of death. It's located three inches below the belly button. It relates to the reproductive system.

The crystals for this are snowflake obsidian, carnelian, and orange calcite. Aromatherapy for this chakra is sweet orange, rose, ylang ylang, frankincense, and davana. Foods that can help with this are carrots, oranges, sweet potatoes, mangos, grapefruits, and papayas. The frequency associated with this is 417 Hz. Try the affirmations I am creative. I respect my body. I trust my feelings. I trust myself.

The third chakra is the **Solar Plexus Chakra.** It's also known as the **Manipura.** It's the color Yellow. It controls our vitality, will power, self-esteem, and self love. It took me forever to distinguish and understand that self-love is not selfish. The organs connected to this are the gallbladder, liver, spleen, pancreas, and the small intestines.

The crystals for this chakra are agate, citrine, yellow jasper and sunstone. The scents for this are lemongrass and myrrh. Suggested foods would include whole wheat, corn, lemon, banana, pineapple, and curry. Some affirmations for this chakra are: I'm powerful. I'm brave. I have a divine purpose. I'm motivated. The frequency for this one is 528 Hz.

The fourth chakra is the **Heart Chakra.** It's also known as the **Anahaus.** Its color is Green. It's our center for unconditional love. It controls the heart, lungs, chest, arms and hands.

Crystals to work with would be emerald, rose quartz, amazonite, moss agate, and peridotite. Try the fragrance of lavender, jasmine and rose. You can eat spinach, peas, broccoli, avocado and limes. It resonates at 639 Hz. For affirmations try I am love. I'm deserving. I attract kind, loving people into my life.

Next, we have the fifth chakra; the **Throat chakra.** It's also known as the **Vishuddha.** Its color is Blue. It's linked to the endocrine and thyroid systems and the neck, ears, mouth, teeth, and gums. It's responsible for communications, self-expressions, and listening skills.

The best crystals for this are lapis lazuli, blue lace agate, aquamarine, celestite, azurite, and amazite. Smells to consider would be peppermint, chamomile and blue tansy. The best foods for this are blueberries, blackberries, and plums. Its frequency is 741 Hz. Affirmations for this I speak my truths. I listen to my inner knowledge. I do no harm with my words.

The sixth chakra is the **Third Eye Chakra.** It's also known as the **Ajna.** It's located between the brow in the middle of the forehead. It's the color Purple. It's directly linked to the pineal gland, melatonin production, and circulatory system. It controls perception and spiritual awareness. It's the light of the body. If unbalanced you may get disturbing visions.

Matthew 6:22 "If the eye be single, the whole body shall be filled with light." The best crystals for this are labradorite, amethyst, solidite and clear quartz. Its scents are juniper, marjoram, patchouli, and vetiver. The foods associated with this are cacao, goji berries, watermelons, cilantro, ginsign, vitamin D3, honey, and coconut oil. Its frequency is 852 Hz. Affirmations are: I embrace wisdom. I'm aligned. I believe in the power of my imagination.

I suggest pure tones when listening to frequency. Using headphones is also extremely helpful. You don't need to meditate while using them. You can simply put them on and do household chores. I would also recommend that you balance the first five chakras prior to attempting to open your third eye. If you're not grounded, this could be an unpleasant experience if you're not prepared.

I would also suggest once the first five are spinning correctly to try a breathing exercise to help activate your pineal gland. There are small crystals inside and it helps to get them vibrating. Breathe into your root. Bring the breath through all your other chakras by contracting the muscles corresponding with them. Once you reach the third eye hold it for 15-20 seconds. Then slowly release your breath.

There's contradicting evidence, however, I believe it's worth a mention–the pineal gland is said to produce small amounts of DMT (Dimethyltryptamine). This is the active ingredient in acid. I've never had this experience.

The last one we will discuss is the **Crown Chakra.** It's also called the **Sahasrara.** It's a violet-white glowing color. It's our connection to God or higher consciousness. It can take a lifetime to activate this chakra. It's directly linked to our brain and nervous system.

The crystals best for this are clear quartz, fluorite, lepidolite, and amethyst. The scents are everlasting flowers, spikenard, galbanum, and cedarwood. The foods are mushrooms, garlic, ginger, and onion. It resonates at 963 Hz. The best affirmations are I am aware of the Divine within. I am open to new ideas. The information I need comes easily to me.

I know, especially in the Christian church, that there are discrepancies over the use of crystals. Let's look to the Bible to help with this.

Exodus 28:17 it's regarding Aaron's breastplate. "Then mount four rows of precious stones. The first row shall be carnelian, chrysolite, and beryl. The second row shall be turquoise, lapis lazuli, and emerald. The third row shall be jacinth, agate, and amethyst. The fourth row shall be topaz, onyx and jasper. Mount them in gold filigree settings. There are to be twelve stones; one for each of the sons of Israel. Engraved like a seal with the name of each of the twelve tribes."

Why would God assign these for Aaron to wear if he never intended for us to use them?

The Bible doesn't go into the energy properties of crystals. However, they definitely hold frequencies. They are used in modern day technology by applying alternating voltage to the crystals. It creates mechanical vibrations. The cut and size determines the resonant frequency of these vibrations or oscillations and can generate a constant signal. They can be found in clear quartz watches, inkjet printers, liquid crystal display screens, sonar, record players and radio transmitters, just to name a few. When I discovered this, it really made me wonder how much more there is that we're not made readily aware of.

It really makes no difference how you prefer to activate and balance your chakras. It's an individual preference. You can experiment with all the different ways and decide what works best for you. You'll know either energetically or emotionally when you have achieved this.

CHAPTER 2.6 LINGUISTICS OF THE LORD'S PRAYER

If you're having trouble accepting the message of The Lord's Prayer because of religious dogma I completely understand. This was a tremendous struggle within myself. I kept going back and forth. I often question whether or not even learning about this was against God. I know it's different from what the churches typically teach. I had an insatiable desire to find the truth and my inner-knowing guided me to learning about this is Jesus' own language. It would be Aramaic.

The letter J didn't exist in his language. The man we refer to as Jesus would actually be called Yeshua. When I read the Bible, I looked at our King James Version, and then translated Aramaic. One of the biggest differences I found is in Matthew 6:9-13

In the King James Version it states, "In this manner therefore pray. Our Father in heaven, hallowed be thy name. Your kingdom comes; your will be done on earth as it is in heaven. Give us this day your daily bread and forgive our debts and we forgive our debtors. don't deliver us into temptation. Deliver us from evil. For yours is the power and glory forever. Amen"

In first century Aramaic, it reads, "Oh thou from the breath of life comes, who fills all realms with sound, light, and vibration.

May your light be experienced in my utmost holiness. Your heavenly domain approaches. Let your will come true in the universe (all the vibrates) just as on earth (that is material and dense). Give us wisdom, understanding and help for our daily needs. Detach the fetters of fault that bind us (karma). Like we let go of the guilt of others. Let us not be lost in superficial things but let us be freed from what keeps us off our true purpose. From you comes thy all working will, the living strength to act, the song that beautifies all and renews itself from age to age. Sealed in trust, faith and truth."

As you can see, Yeshua was obviously aware of the fact that light, sound, and vibration creates our reality. Scientists now can finally mathematically prove this as well through quantum physics. Religion and science have always been on opposite sides, but now they're on the same page. The possibilities of what this could mean are limitless.

New Age teaches that we're moving into the Fifth dimension;

Which is more of a state of mind rather than a physical location. A state of unconditional love over fear. Regardless of your personal thoughts on the New Age spiritual movement, if everyone lives in a state of non-judgement and unequivocal love, we will have the positive, desired outcome that will help change the world. Remember, reality is only real through the lens of the observer. As real or imagined as this may sound, it makes absolutely no difference. Security, love, and acceptance is all we genuinely desire.

I've touched on manifestation, the law of attraction, which simply is matching vibrations. A simple example of how to do this would be that you want a Lexus. First, you'd imagine the car, its colors, the features you want in it, and even the smell. Feel what it would be like to drive in it. Don't hold back; get excited. Then you need to put in an action. This is how you are communicating with the great Spirit. So, in this example go to the dealership to look for the one you want. You could even take a test drive. Then the hardest part is letting it go. Stop worrying about it and trust that what your heart desires is on the way.

The combination of thought, feeling, action, and trust makes room to bring in the desire. Don't worry about how it will come, just trust that it will. I can give numerous examples of this in my life. I'll share a simple, almost silly example. I had learned about the health benefits of seaweed. I learned about its nutritional value. I came up with a recipe that I would put the seaweed in. I couldn't find it at the local store. It wasn't a big deal, so I forgot about it. A month or so later we were low on food and money and needed to go to the food bank. Low and behold; what was in the box? Seaweed. This was extremely unlikely. Too much so to be a coincidence.

Also, we all consistently manifest unconsciously. Most of the time we manifest negative experiences for ourselves. If we're going to manifest regardless, why not consciously manifest a preferred experience instead? Not only do we manifest on an individual level but on a collective level as well. If everyone truly understood how this worked, we could legitimately create an exceptional world for everyone.

The rulers, the one percent elite, of this world are absolutely aware of this. This is why our media, movies and even music is filled with so much negativity, sexuality, and fear. They get a majority of the population thinking, acting and feeling in a pessimistic state. That keeps our vibrations low and gives them their desired result.

CHAPTER 2.7 UNIVERSAL LAWS

I have briefly shown you how the universal laws work in everyday life. What are the laws? Where did they come from? They aren't written by man but discovered by observation and experience.

The Law of Oneness

We are all connected to everyone and everything around us. Our actions affect everyone and everything around us. This can be referred to as God, Source, the field, or zeropoint. Think about string theory.

The Law of Vibration

Everything in the universe moves, vibrates, and travels in a circular pattern. This applies to the physical as well as the etheric realm. Every person, sound, object and even thought creates its own vibrational frequency which is unique to itself.

The Law of Action

This law must be applied to manifest anything here in the third dimension. We must take action to bring forth any dream.

The Law of Correspondence

This explains that the physical world, made of light, sound, and vibration, have a corresponding principle in the etheric realm. Hence the saying; As above so below.

The Law of Cause and Effect

Nothing happened by chance or outside of these laws. Every action has a reaction. You reap what you sow. This would be called karma. Karma can be positive or negative depending on the corresponding actions.

The Law of Compensation

This applies to blessings and gifts that are provided for us. This is the visible effects of our deeds. Do good; get good.

The Law of Attractions

This law demonstrates how we create things, events, and even people coming into our life. Our thoughts, feelings, and actions produce energy. This in turn attracts like energy. Positive attracts positive just as negative attracts negative.

The Law of Perpetual Transmutation of Energy

This is a very powerful one. It states that all persons have the power to change their life. Higher vibrations transform and consume lower ones. We all have the power to transform our lives by understanding and effectively applying all the Universal Laws.

The Law of Relativity

This law states that each and every person will have a series of problems or tests of initiation. This is done to strengthen the light within. We must see these problems to only be challenges. We should stay connected to our hearts when proceeding to solve the problems by observing these dilemmas with proper perception.

The Law of Polarity

Everything is on a continuum and has an opposite. This is represented by the Yin/yang symbol. We can transform any negative, undesirable thought by concentrating on its polar opposite. It's the law of mental vibration.

The Law of Rhythm

This states that everything moves and vibrates at a certain rhythm. These rhythms establish our seasons, cycles, stages of development, and patterns. Each reflecting God's regularity and stability in our universe. Mastering this can allow us to rise above negative cycles by never getting overly worked up or never allowing negative things to penetrate our consciousness.

The Law of Gender

Everything has its masculine (Yin) and feminine (Yang) principles. These are the basis for all creation. Once you balance the Yin and Yang, you have earned the right to be a spiritual co-creator.

This is the duality of the dark and the light which is inside everything. We have to find a balance between the two or they will be constantly chasing one another. This symbol is actually called the Taijitu. It has come to represent Taoism.

The Yin is associated with the female aspect. It's represented by darkness, nighttime and the moon. Her qualities are contemplation, quiet, contraction, and stillness.

The Yang is associated with the masculine. He is represented as the sun. He can be bright, limitless, and even at times reckless. Think about action, expansion, growth and movement.

An example in nature would be an egg. The eggshell is the Yin whereas the Yang would be the yoke. We contain both inside of us. The goal is to balance both. Taoism is more of a principle than a religion. I see correlations to this and the universal laws.

CHAPTER 2.8 SPIRITUAL AWAKENING STAGES

My goal in writing this book is twofold. Primarily, my intention is to show through truth, openness, and honesty who I truly am as a person and how I got here in order to show others they can do the same. I've had an initiation of problems that I have overcome. I was truly blessed with the gift of Grace. The gift of Grace is given not by what you have done, but because you're going to be used to help others to bring forth their own light. I'm forever grateful for this gift.

The second reason for writing this book is that spiritual awakenings can be intense and sometimes frightening. When this happened to me, very little was available about this or I didn't know where to look. I'm attempting to simplify the information for anyone who's struggling or searching for encouragement. Enlightenment is a life-changing process. When you've been awakened, there's no going back.

I've come to understand that we're amidst Christ's return. It's not necessarily in the sky. It's happening inside of all of us. At some point in this lifetime, EVERYONE will be presented with the opportunity to bring the energy of Christ's light into our hearts through unconditional love, acceptance, and forgiveness.

Spiritual awakening happens in stages. These stages don't usually occur in any specific order. I can assure you that you're not going crazy. There are coaches that are great supporters. If you're anything like me, this option might not be in your budget. If having professional support is a challenge, finding a mentor could be a solution.

In Matthew 19:30, Jesus says, "Many who are first will be last and the last may come first." I can see this happening in my personal life. Not just for myself, but also the ones around me that have begun to awaken. Most people I know who are learning to understand what's going on are those who have been diagnosed with mental problems, struggled with addiction, and/or have a lot of childhood trauma. They are the black sheep. The ones our society, unfortunately, considers last.

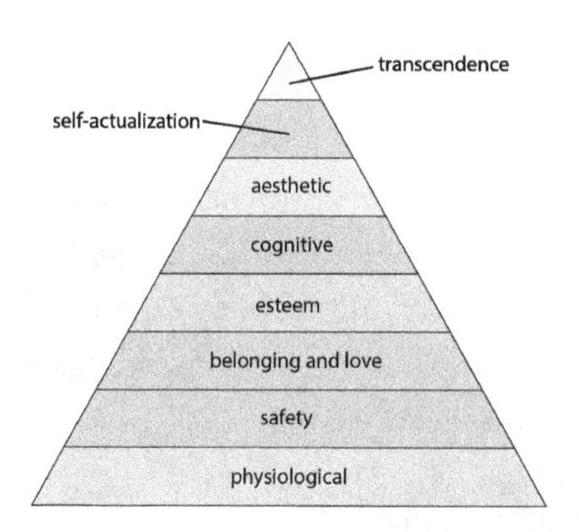

Maslow's Hierarchy of Needs is an accurate visual to how our society is structured. It's easy to see how we get stuck in the lower two categories. Our society hasn't been set up for self-actualization. We struggle most of our lives to make enough money to have physiological needs appropriately met such as shelter, food, and clothing. If we get lucky enough to have a medium class income, we may make it to a place where we can establish safety through financial security, resources, own property, and caring for our health properly. So, how are we ever supposed to climb to self-actualize?

I believe the best solution for this is the "why" this is all happening the way it is. Like I just stated, the Bible says "the last will come first ." So, if the bottom two layers were to spontaneously awaken, then it would cause the whole pyramid to come falling down. This would give us an equal playing field for everyone. Once you start to self-actualize, you'll come to learn that your needs will always be met. We live on our Mother Earth. When the Earth is cared for properly, the abundance in the land will sustain our needs.

Fredrich Nietzsche, a German philosopher, once said "Once awake, you shall remain awake eternally." This is very accurate and also representative of the common beginning stages of spiritual awakening.

A Spark of Awareness

Through Our lifetime we experience many tastes of awakening both big and small. These are marked by moments of clarity; like an "ah ha" moment or have an out-of-body experience. This will cause you to question your existence more personally as well as your place in the whole human collective.

Intense Research

This sudden spark inspires you to want to know more. You'll most likely seek spiritual or ecoscentric knowledge. Your research may include going a little crazy with YouTube videos, buying books and some crystals, or anything that you believe will provide you with answers. Beware of the unlimited rabbit holes this may throw you into. Luckily, during this phase you should learn to develop your intuition and an understanding of the voice of Spirit so that you can discern what you are learning.

Dark Night of the Soul

Sometimes this may be the first phase of an awakening as well. If we have a traumatic event, such as a premature death of a loved one, we may have to reevaluate how we thought our life was going to be. Life may feel meaningless. We experience feelings of numbness and sadness, almost as if we were mourning or experiencing a deep depression. Even if we haven't physically lost someone, that spark of awareness can trigger the feeling of loss, knowing that your life will never be the same. Just as there's no order to this stage, there's no provision for time limits. This may last a few weeks to even a few years. We'll experience this stage multiple times. Don't get discouraged; this too will pass.

Meeting the Shadow Self

At some point we must face our darkness. We have to inspect our shadow; our inner demons. We revisit childhood traumas with a fresh pair of eyes. We can look at others' actions that caused us this pain and see what may have caused them to do what they did. This was a very humbling experience for me. When I went through this, it was extremely intense. My awakening was spontaneous, and I understood the spiritual gifts that were already active. Combine this with my unhealed religious dogma; it was terrifying for me.

When I worked on my inner demons, they appeared. I saw them in dreams literally attempting to possess me. I'd witness them out of the corner of my eye. Sometimes I just knew they were around. The mind plays tricks on us. We create what we believe and that's exactly what I was doing to myself. The more I worked on healing my past, the less frequently these sightings and dreams occurred. I don't think this is very common, however; I want to include this in case there are others struggling with this experience. Another thing I found very helpful is to think of things as pure energy. Getting rid of negative energy is a much more soothing idea whereas fighting demons is ghastly.

No matter what you have to face, embrace your shadow with unconditional love and understanding. Remember your shadow is your ego. It was developed as a self-protection mechanism when you were in a position that you could not protect yourself. Carefully examining each situation and making some sort of peace with them will overcome your darkness. Remember, it's okay to forgive others for creating peace within yourself. Just because you forgive someone doesn't mean that you allow them back in to hurt you again. Not everyone is in the same place that you are and they can't see things the way you do yet and that's okay too.

Integration of Dark and Light within

Our dark and light may also be referred to as the ego and higher self. I'm aware not everyone has an inner monologue. I do. So, I can only share what it's like from this perspective.

My two inner voices often discuss and, argue in my head. I never knew what this was until I began to really tune into myself and observe what was going on in there. Think about the cartoons with an angel on one shoulder and the devil on the other. I've learned to distinguish my higher self from the positive advice that I normally hear on my right side. My ego is the one that causes doubts and I can hear that on my left side. It's different for everyone. There's no right or wrong in any of this. It's more like what feels right for you individually.

Understanding my inner monologue gave me permission to tune more frequently into my higher self and realize my ego was just speaking out of fear. I could then get my ego to understand I'm safe and no longer need that form of protection. I could thank ego for doing its job for so long. Doing this allowed me to venture back into society. I was beginning to discuss my experiences with open-minded individuals that have gone through similar experiences.

Search for Purpose

We're beginning to see that life isn't meaningless. We're not meant to merely be born, go to school, get a job, and hopefully retire a few years before we die just to repeat the cycle in our next lifetime. We desire to reach enlightenment by breaking this pattern.

We can see that life needs to be more in service to others than to self. We seek our place in a physical world that can benefit everyone. To be in the world, but not of it.

Enlightenment

This is alignment within self. We begin to feel a lightness within. Life may not appear to be perfect on the outside but we experience a deep sense of peace and contentment. Our soul, which is actually our higher self, is more fully embodied in our everyday life. We're aware of our spiritual gifts and use them to guide our everyday life.

CHAPTER 2.9 UNDERSTANDING SPIRITUAL GIFTS

Growing up with such a strong Catholic upbringing caused me to fear the unknown. Spiritual gifts were viewed as witchcraft. Mine showed up resembling mental illness. In some ways, it kept me in my addiction. I wanted to stop feeling crazy, so I would keep using. This is common. I've always felt energy and the feelings of others. This made it hard for me to be in large crowds. It made me feel like an outsider.

Rather than learning these were gifts; I saw them as a curse. I often wonder if I had known all of this sooner how different my life would've been. I know now that I wouldn't be who I am today without every one of these experiences.

Today, I choose to see these lessons as blessings. They have taught me empathy and forgiveness. I've been able to learn non-judgement; you never know what else someone is going through. There's no saying what brought them to where they are today. I've learned that most people do their best with where they are mentally and emotionally.

For me, the hardest lesson to finding my blessing was in the pain I caused my children. I'm still working on this. I'm aware this is holding me back from self-confidence. Shadow work is a never-ending process.

When we explore spiritual gifts, they're usually seen from two different sides of the spectrum. On the metaphysical side they are referred to as Claires. From a biblical perspective, they are called Gifts of the Spirit.

The Claires include Clairvoyance, Clairaudience, Clairsentience, Claircognizance, Clairesalience, Clairgustance, Clairtangency, and Clairempathy. In the Bible, the gifts of Spirit are the prophecy, knowledge, wisdom, speaking in tongues, interpretation of tongue, miracles, healing, discernment of spirits, fortitude, and understanding. Each of us is given a unique combination of these. It states in Acts 10:34, "God does not show favoritism." We all have spiritual gifts; it's up to us to discover what they are and develop them.

I've researched and compared these gifts. I can see similarities in a lot of them. There are at least four that I can positively discern to be the same.

Clairvoyance means clear seeing. This is what you would consider being a psychic in our times. In the Bible, this is the gift of prophecy. It's listed amongst the gifts in 1Corithians 14. From my understanding, we're given these gifts to help others. If we become too prideful or use them solely for personal gain, we lose them. They're gifts and should be treated with reverence.

Clairaudience is clear hearing. It's recognizing that inner voice of truth. This appears as wisdom in the Bible.

Clairsentient is clear feeling. We may appear to be overly emotional until we understand this gift. You feel too much all the time. You may have trouble in large crowds. This is actually understanding. Once you learn how to separate your true feelings from those around you, you'll feel the energy of the physical or possibly the etheric world around you.

This is the perfect chance for you to work on your discernment of spirit. 1 John 4:1-6 says "Beloved, believe not every spirit. But try the spirits to see whether they are God. Because many prophets have gone out into the world." In today's times, especially with the internet, we need to be very careful of others' intentions. We need to discern the information we're hearing, regardless of the source, and feel how it sits with you. Is the information off or is your programming off? Listen to your heart instead of your mind. Is the person or information coming from a place of love? After all, God is Love.

Claircognizance is clear knowing. This gift is an instinctive knowing of a thing, but have no idea how you came to know it. This is referred to in the Bible as the gift of knowledge. Each of our gifts have the ability to strengthen either with practice or supernaturally. The gift of knowledge should be used with the gift of wisdom to help others.

Clairempathy to strengthen either through practice or supernaturally. The gift of knowledge should be u is clear emotions. It means you have the ability to tune into the emotions of people, places and even animals. This can also occur across time and space. Basically, you are feeling the frequency of their auras and learning to interpret them. Obviously, this is empathy in the Bible.

Clairesalience is clear smelling. I'm not all that familiar with this one. An example of this would be smelling the perfume of a loved one who's passed away.

Clairgustance is clear tasting. An example of this would be driving by a field of strawberries and literally being able to taste them.

Clairtangency is a clear touch. With this you can feel and identify the energies of an object. You may be able to see or sense the memories it holds.

The other biblical gifts are speaking in tongues and interpretation of tongues. This has been made visibly available with the popularity of the internet. Individuals are speaking unknown languages and using hand gestures. It is more recently referred to as light language.

We must not leave out the gift of miracles or the gift of healing. I have experienced both of these numerous times in my life. My life has literally been saved numerous times from overdoses. I've had my liver disease disappear as well as the tumor in my sinus cavity. Not everyone that is a healer, does so for disease. We can heal ourselves and others, both mentally and emotionally, often by being there in times of need. This ultimately prevents disease (dis-ease). Our gifts are given to us using a variety of forms and degrees. The more grateful we are for them, the more we are given.

CHAPTER 2.10 THE BEGINNING OF DISCLOSURE

Chapter 2.10 The Beginning of Disclosure

God/Source is all and created all. John 1:3 states, "All things were made through Him, without Him nothing was made." This would mean God created everything, or you could even say that God is the Universe. There are ten to twelve dimensions in our universe depending on which source you research or if you're looking at this from a spiritual or scientific point of view.

I'm going to attempt to give a combination explanation to the best of my understanding. The twelve dimensions are broken into four realms. This is explained in Ezekiel's wheel.

In it states Ezekiel 10:10-14. "And as for their appearance, they four had one likeness, as if the wheel had been amidst a wheel. When they went they went upon their four sides; they turned not as they went, but to the way their head looked they followed it; they turned not as they went. And their whole body, their backs, and their hands, and their wings and their wheels, were full of eyes roundabout, even the wheels that they four had. As for the wheels, it cried into my hearing, oh wheel. Everyone had four faces; the first face was the face of a cherub, and the second was the face of a man, and the third face that of a lion, the fourth face that of an eagle."

This is used to symbolize our universe; our connection to all in this life and our after life. The realm of the human would be Dimensions One through Three. Dimension one is best described as a straight line on a piece of paper, length, or unconsciousness. Dimension Two would be a vertical line; which gives us the ability to make a shape such as a square. This could also be seen as subconscious. Dimension Three would be depth; a sense of area like a cube. This would include all physical dense matter.

The realm of the lion would be Dimensions Four through Six. In these realms, we'd have a sense of peace. Beings would be physically and mentally stronger. There would be unity consciousness; similar to lions in a pack. The ability to see the future would be present to help in making decisions. The Fourth Dimension is time like plotting a position in the universe. This is the astral realm. Beings here have rainbow bodies, physic power, and a transitional mind. Thoughts and emotions can be created here. The Fifth Dimension would be a world slightly different from ours. Beings here would have a Christ-like mind. They are ascended beings that can create with thought almost instantly. The Sixth Dimension would be a plane of all the possible worlds that were created with the same start like the big bang for example. Time travel amongst those worlds is possible hereby the use of Mekabra. Beings here have a cosmic consciousness. Full souls take life and form here.

The next realms would be that of the eagle. It's the realm with the bird's-eye view. Here you can see the past and all future timelines existing at once. This would be Dimensions Seven through Nine. Dimension Seven would be a plane where all worlds can be seen regardless of their initial beginning conditions. It is the domain of souls. The I AM resides here. Dimension Eight is where all the different worlds, timelines, and planes branch out infinitely. It holds all geometric codes, the administration angels, and the brotherhood of lights. The Ninth Dimension is where all the universe's possible histories with different laws of physics and beginning conditions can be compared. This is like a planning administration or planetary logos. The dimension of Archangels and Elohim.

The last is a spiritual domain, the Realm of the Cherubin. This is the closest to God/Source. It contains Dimensions Ten through Twelve. The Tenth Dimension is the point of all possibilities and imagination. The dimensions of oversouls and the birthplace of individualized souls. It is pure radiance and color. The Eleventh Dimension is the universal plan. It contains the plan codes, universal laws and harmonics. One thousand aspects of spirit/archangels and the creator counsel are here. The Twelfth Dimension is God/ Source.

Dimensions are different facets of our perceived reality. They're not necessarily physical locations, but rather levels of consciousness. Think about it like a lasagna layers upon layers of different existence making up one. This is the best way I can explain with Third dimensional thinking and knowledge. To think that humans are the only life form in such inconceivable vastness is almost laughable.

So much has been hidden from us. Possibly, humanity's consciousness wasn't ready for this awareness. A lot can be found in our ancient sites. From Egypt to South America, writings and drawings show spaceships and depict technology we just now have available.

There are endless sightings common to those similar to those seen by the Kyiv Astronomical Observatory. They have witnessed hundreds of UAP's, Unidentified Aerial Phenomenon, flying over Ukraine on September 15, 2022. There is no coincidence that an increased amount of beings are seen during war times.

The United States Intelligence Committee had an open forum meeting on May 15, 2022. Here the Pentagon admits to over four hundred verified sightings and eleven actual encounters. In August of 2022, they started a UAP task force to take reports and investigate all sightings and encounters.

Lisa Eisenhower, the great granddaughter of the president, alleges that in 1954 he was approached by two, maybe three different groups of extraterrestrials. The first being Lord Valent from the planet Venus; who offered a plan for world peace and the end to famine and illness? After reviewing it he decided against it because of the impact it would have on the United States financial economy. Instead he made a deal with the Gray's for weapons and technology for allowing a few human abductions.

It amazes me at all the very recent discoveries of "lost" cities. The lost city of Luxor in Egypt that was covered for three thousand years. On July 1, 2022 they found a two thousand year old temple in the Netherlands. On July 22,2022 A Hellenistic theater dating to 2 BC was discovered in Thera, Turkey. A five thousand year old Neolithic chambered tomb was discovered in Herefordshire, England. It's believed to belong to the King Author. On January 24, 2022 thousands of prehistoric pits were found at Stonehenge.

In China, due to receding rivers thirty one Buddhist statues that were over six hundred years old were found. As well as a sinkhole that contained a large forest with its own ecosystem. Two hundred mummies in Egypt in the Saqqara were unearthed. These all just scratch the surface of the findings and goes to show that Revelations simply means the revealing. Can you imagine what information all these discoveries will produce?

Is the idea of other life forms really that far fetch when we're now just scratching the surface of things on our own planet? Disclosure is happening everywhere. It just isn't being publicized by our television stations.

You may or may not have come across the New Age idea of Starseeds or Light workers. This is coming from many past life regressions that all unknowingly tell the same story. Dolorase Cannon was one of the first to come across this. She and others were told during these sessions that God/Source saw that our world was desperately in the need of change. The destruction of Earth would have a ripple effect throughout the universe. This isn't allowed to happen. Instead of allowing the Earth to be destroyed again, He put a call out to souls incarnated all over this universe and others. He asked for souls to volunteer to incarnate during this time. This would include a soul contract that included a traumatic childhood in order for the soul to awaken and remember their purpose. It would also provide them a chance to work off karma faster than normal. What would usually take multiple lifetimes to erase could be fulfilled in a single lifetime. Tragically, a good amount of the first wave of volunteers ended up committing suicide or overdosing before they even discovered their purpose. Earth in the Third Dimension is very dense. From what I've heard, these souls started incarnating after World War II.

To me, reincarnation has always made sense. Energy can't be created or destroyed. One lifetime can't possibly provide enough time to experience everything we need for our soul to grow. If we all are truly fractals of God/Source experiencing itself, then it makes sense to gather all the experiences we can.

It's disputed in Christian communities but why would life only be created on Earth? Some even believe aliens are demons. I choose to keep my vibration high and refuse to buy into this claim. Just like there are good and bad people, I believe the same applies to extraterrestrials or even interdimensional, as I prefer to call them. Maybe the words are interchangeable; demons are negative agenda ET's whereas Angels are higher-level beings. Since a lot of these beings are etheric. I look at them as energy without a physical existence.

We learned in the Universal Law of transmutation that high vibrations absorb and consume lower ones. When I get bothered by lower frequencies, I ground and send them down to Mother Earth to be transformed into positive ones. Just like we breathe in oxygen and breathe out carbon dioxide, the trees breathe in carbon dioxide and exhale the oxygen we need. The earth does this type of exchange with energies. I'm amazed how interconnected everything is in the universe.

This interconnectedness goes beyond all time and space. It's what enables us to communicate with our spirit guides, our ancestors, and angels. Yes, we all have them. Some are even what we would consider extraterrestrial.

Have you ever wondered why we have twelve strains of DNA and are told nine of them are junk? This information never sat right with me. I believe that there will soon be a discovery or revelation that the other strands are laying dormant and through our awakening process this DNA will also awaken. If you have the mind to view the Adam and Eve story through an ancient astronaut theorist lens it will reveal a completely different story. The tale accounts an interdimensional race manipulating our DNA. Summarian text highly suggests it was the Annunaki race. I believe they weren't the only ones. This essentially makes us a combination of many extraterrestrial races.

If this were true in theory and the "junk" DNA becomes activated, think about all the possibilities and superhuman powers we would have. Let your imagination work out that vision!

Princeton University has actually done a study showing how pieces of our once-thought-to-be-useless DNA can act as on/off switches for our genes. The study was published in the "Journal of Nature Genetics."

It's really going to be an exciting ride we're all in for. There are so many more topics to be explored. I can't give you all the answers as I'm still seeking for myself. I hoped to help guide you through my process and hopefully provide you with some basic information I wish I had. If you've read this book, you most likely have a bigger purpose in this lifetime as well.

I wish I could tell you how this is all going to play out, but we don't get those answers–we get the answers we need and even those will bring about more questions. It may take a while to find your purpose. Sometimes, your purpose is to hold the light for others to awaken. Since linear time only exists here, I can assure you no matter how dark it gets the light has already won. In the here and now, we are witnessing it all unfold. We are safe. We are protected. We are loved.

I give everyone a big Congratulations! You made it to graduation!!! It's no small feat for the soul. Remember, it's a journey and not a destination. It's not all love and light all the time. Life will most definitely have its ups and downs. Just doing the inner work, the reward of internal peace is definitely worth it.

NOTES

I believe we all have a part in this. I would love to be a support anyone in need. Feel free to email me for guidance or to connect at myaberrantmind@gmail.com

CPSIA information can be obtained
at www.ICGtesting.com
Printed in the USA
JSHW012125050323
38430JS00005B/169